Formula 1 Paddock

Jean-Francois Galeron

CHRONOSPORTS
EDITEUR

ISBN 2-84707-046-X

Jordils Park, Chemin des Jordils 40,
CH-1025 St-Sulpice,
SWITZERLAND
Tel.: (+41 21 694 24 44)
Fax: (+41 21 694 24 46)
E-mail: info@chronosports.com
www.chronosports.com

Design, page layout, Jacket Designer and
production Manager: Cyril Davillerd

Printed and bound in Italy.

Formula 1 Paddock

Photographies and words
Jean-Francois Galeron

Art Director
Cyril Davillerd

CHRONOSPORTS
EDITEUR

CONTENTS

CHAPTER 1

BEHIND THE SCENES

CHAPTER 2

PADDOCK LIFE

CHAPTER 3

THE MEDIA

CHAPTER 4

THE PEOPLE

FOREWORD by
Bernie ECCLESTONE

After fifty legendary years, Formula 1 has never been in such good health. The intensity of competition has attracted the greatest names in the world of motoring. Thus in 2002, we have gladly welcomed Renault and Toyota, two new major manufacturers.

While hundreds of thousands of TV viewers admire the Formula 1 "show," in actual fact, they only see the tip of the iceberg. At each grand prix, over 10,000 people work behind the scenes in a variety of roles to bring your favourite sport to your television screens.

Jean-Francois Galeron, a photographer in this exciting environment for over 20 years, has chosen to bring you a glimpse of what goes on in a Formula 1 paddock, in words and pictures.

Some of these people will be well known to you, as they have worked hard to make Formula 1 one what it is today, but you will also learn about all the little details which go to make up the paddock, which is a closed and unknown world to the vast majority of fans.

The book contains over 800 photos and a large number of interviews, which will give you a privileged view behind the scenes, allow you to enter the motorhomes and let you discover all those places you have dreamt of exploring. You will meet the media and the team personnel. They will explain every facet of their fascinating jobs.

Welcome to the Formula 1 Paddock.

Bernie Ecclestone

INTRODUCTION

The name paddock has its origins as a place where horses are kept and motor racing adopted this word to define the area behind the pits where the trucks, cars and motorhomes are parked. It is the nerve centre of the race circuit.

In the past, all spectators were allowed into the paddock to meet the drivers and see the cars. Then, an entrance fee was charged and although the cost was often prohibitive, there was always a huge crowd of fans keen to enter the inner sanctum to meet their heroes. This led to the decision to quite simply ban the public from the Formula 1 paddock. For a few years, the real fans would always find a way in, illegally dealing with fences that were not particularly robust. However, for the past five years, an electronic system controls all entries into this area with the electronic gates guarding the only entry to the paddock. Everyone has to go through the swipe machine, be they drivers, engineers, mechanics or journalists. Powerful computers control the swipe gates, so that everyone's movements can be monitored.

Hence, the Formula 1 paddock has become a Forbidden City. Some lucky fans can still get in, courtesy of the Formula One Paddock Club to see just part of this marvellous world in idyllic conditions. At all the circuits around the world, fans are pressed up against the fencing for a glimpse of this fascinating and mysterious world.

For over twenty years, my job means I am allowed through the gates. I have never taken it for granted and am always excited every time I step inside a world which all race fans dream of.

Here you have the third edition of "Formula 1 Paddock" The first two editions came out in 2000 and 2002, in French only. But in this world, it is not just the cars which go quickly and some of the characters have moved on to be replaced by new ones. In the paddock, the setting for this book, everything moves at the speed of light.

In these pages I will try and provide an insight into this incredible world of high technology, which one does not see often in the pages of magazines or on television. It is Formula 1 seen from the paddock.

1 BEHIND THE SCENES

chapter 1

BEHIND THE SCENES

These days, it is very difficult to get into the paddock. Spectators dream of crossing its threshold. The team motorhomes and trucks constitute a sparkling window on the world of Formula 1. Now you can stroll around at your leisure and explore this magical world.

30 years ago

The French Grand Prix at Clermont-Ferrand in 1972.

The Lotus mechanics prepare Emerson Fittipaldi's car for the French Grand Prix at Clermont-Ferrand in 1972.

Under the McLaren truck awning in 1975.

The BRM transporter at the French Grand Prix at Clermont-Ferrand in 1972.

The Tyrrell team at the 1972 French
Grand Prix at Clermont-Ferrand.

The paddock at the Montjuich Park circuit near Barcelona in 1973.

The McLaren team at the 1972 French
Grand Prix at Clermont-Ferrand.

The Matra team at the 1968 French Grand Prix at Rouen.

Generalview
of the
paddock....

Zeltweg in 1978.

The first Renault motorhome at Silverstone in 1977.

The look of the paddock has changed beyond recognition. In the 50s and the early 60s, the only vehicles in the paddock were the team trucks. It was only in the 70s that the paddocks were asphalted. At Charade, near Clermont-Ferrand for example, the trucks and cars were parked behind the pits in a mowed field. The back of the trucks was the only place for the drivers to relax. Deck chairs, camping tables and chairs were the sum total of the furniture available.

It was only in 1964, on a suggestion from photo-journalist Bernard Cahier, who looked after press relations for Goodyear, that the first mobile home made its appearance. It

The McLaren
motorhome in the
foreground at the
Spa-Francorchamps
circuit in 1984.

View of the Dijon-Prenois
paddock in 1982.

Jerez de la Frontera in 1986.

Budapest in 1991.

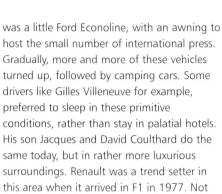

was a little Ford Econoline, with an awning to
host the small number of international press.
Gradually, more and more of these vehicles
turned up, followed by camping cars. Some
drivers like Gilles Villeneuve for example,
preferred to sleep in these primitive
conditions, rather than stay in palatial hotels.
His son Jacques and David Coulthard do the
same today, but in rather more luxurious
surroundings. Renault was a trend setter in
this area when it arrived in F1 in 1977. Not

The Elf motorhome at the end of the Eighties.

This aerial shot of the Magny-Cours paddock gives a good impression of the precision with which all the motorhomes and trucks are lined up.

The Barcelona paddock in 2003.

The Imola paddock in 2003.

The Kuala Lumpur paddock in 2003.

only did the French constructor come up with the revolutionary turbocharged engine, it was also the first company to turn up with a bus, fully kitted out to host the press and team members.

Then, in the 80s, the paddock was invaded by American style motorhomes like Winnebagos,

with all the teams going down this route. Specialist companies transformed these vehicles to order. They had a luxuriously appointed lounge, meeting rooms, rest rooms, a kitchen area and a toilet. Under the awning, tables were laid out to welcome, guests, team members and the press.

Inexorably, year after year the paddock vehicles got ever larger and more luxurious. Even though several of the smaller teams went under, the motorhomes of the bigger teams filled the space available. These days, each team has several motor homes, which seem to be ever bigger. ■

The Imola paddock alongside the river.

On the road to a GrandPrix

2003.04.15

04:00

04:45

Tuesday, 15th April 2003

03h45: Truck drivers arrive at factory

04h00: Cases and three cars loaded into two trucks,

04h30: Loading finished

04h45: The two Sauber trucks leave the factory. The weather is cold and dry.

06h05: Queuing at the St. Gotthard tunnel.

06h30: Going through the tunnel, 100 kms after leaving Hinwil at an average speed of 57 km/h over mountain roads.

06:05

06h45: It starts to rain.

07h20: Breakfast break at the Movenpick restaurant in Bellinzonna.

07h50: On the road again, heading for Lugano and the Italian border.

08h45: The border at Chiasso and time to check the carnets.

09h15: Customs.

09h50: Milan peage, heading for Bologna. It is pouring with rain and there are lots of traffic jams on the Milan ring road near Modena.

12h40: Lunch at the Autogrill restaurant on Bologna's Tangenziale.

13h30: Refuelling the trucks and generators.

13h45: Heading for Imola.

14h20: Imola motorway exit and the trucks head for the track.

14h30: Arrival at the circuit, time to wash the trucks.

15h30: Queuing to get into the paddock.

19h30: The drivers leave the circuit to go to the hotel. It has taken a long time to park up some other team trucks, so they decide to delay moving in until the next day.

Wednesday 16th April 2003

07h45: Parking in the paddock and unloading the cars and equipment.

In brief...

• The two Sauber trailers are pulled by Mercedes Actros tractor units, putting out 460 horsepower. Each unit weighs 32 tonnes.

• Silvan Ruegg and Marco Held take turns at the wheel of the truck carrying the race cars, registration number ZH 801069.

• Bruno Rohr and Christian Scherrer drive the other truck with all the equipment, registration ZH 462102.

• Another trailer had left the day before with all the pit set-up equipment.

• Hinwil to Imola is a distance of 534 kilometres.
• The average speed was 66.1 km/h.
• The journey took 9 hours 45 minutes including stops.
• Diesel consumption was 31.8 litres per 100 kilometres
• The Sauber trucks are limited to a top speed of 90 km/h.
• Each driver is only allowed to do 4 hours behind the wheel before a break.

The Freight

For events outside Europe, all the equipment is transported by air or by sea in huge containers. The chassis are stripped down, with wings and other parts removed.

RALF SCHUMACHER

The Trucks

Ferrari truck in 1964.

Ferrari trucks in 2003.

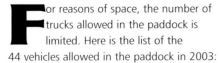

For reasons of space, the number of trucks allowed in the paddock is limited. Here is the list of the 44 vehicles allowed in the paddock in 2003:

- 4 trucks Ferrari including 2 with expandable trailers.
- 3 trucks McLaren including 2 with expandable trailer.
- 1 truck Illmor-Mercedes
- 3 trucks Williams including 1 with expandable trailer.
- 1 truck BMW
- 2 trucks Sauber
- 1 truck Petronas (engine)
- 2 trucks Jordan
- 1 truck Ford
- 2 trucks BAR with expandable trailers.
- 1 truck Honda
- 4 trucks Renault
- 3 trucks Jaguar
- 3 trucks Minardi
- 3 trucks Toyota of which 1 with expandable trailer.
- 4 trucks Bridgestone
- 4 trucks Michelin
- 2 trucks FIA one with awning.

With space being limited, several teams opt for trucks which expand to two levels. A hydraulic system raises an additional level used for the technical briefings.

BAR was the first to use this system, followed by BMW, Ferrari, McLaren and Toyota.

Each team has an air conditioned meeting and technical briefing room in one of the trucks. One of the Ferrari trucks is used exclusively for this purpose. The trucks are packed with computers and measuring and checking devices. A permanent satellite links data from the track to the team's factory.

The fleet of trucks used at the grands prix by each team at the European races is an impressive sight. The equipment needed to set up some of the motorhomes and the sophisticated infrastructure of the garages involves several thirty tonne semi-trailers.

McLaren uses up to 15 trucks, including a refrigerated unit for the catering requirements. Ferrari and Williams make do with 13 units, of which two are solid trucks. BAR and Toyota use 10 and 9 articulated trucks each.

The teams also bring scooters along for short journeys and for driver use. For example, Jacques Villeneuve, David Coulthard and Jenson Button all stay in their own motorhomes at the European races and use the scooters to commute to the paddock. For some time now, two wheeled transport has been banned from the paddock, so they are all neatly lined up at the paddock gate.

Williams' trucks.

The McLaren and Williams mechanics unload all the equipment out of the trucks, which are then cleaned from top to toe.

Inside the McLaren workshop truck.

The double decker trucks which are the latest F1 fashion, can cost up to 1.5 million Euro. They are fitted out with offices, a satellite link and even engine analysis facilities. The interior fit is what can make the price vary on a truck or motorhome. It is hard to put a price on the actual vehicles as they are all one-offs and therefore pretty much prototypes.

The same cleaning procedure goes on for all the teams, such as Renault and Jaguar.

The cheapest trailer comes in at around 15000 Euro, which is also roughly the cost of a tractor unit. These are often supplied free of charge, by manufacturers keen to exploit the publicity value of Formula 1.

Outside the paddock, one finds the Shell, Petrobras, Castrol, Elf-Total and Exon-Mobil trucks which bring the fuel for the various teams.

In 2003 at Imola, the McLaren team once again caused a stir. A year after launching its palatial Communications Centre, the silver team turned up with a new type of transporter. Three of their total of four, those for the engineers, spare parts and the Mercedes Ilmor unit, are now of the double

decker variety. Once parked up, the upper section lifts into place, creating another level with an aluminium and composite floor. The transporter which carries the cars is of the conventional type. As is the case with the motorhomes, the only way to get round the space limitation is to build upwards. This doubles the work surface for engineers and mechanics. On the road, the trucks return to their conventional appearance and the hydraulic system is only used once the vehicle is in the paddock. All the offices in these three units are kitted out with the latest technology and air conditioning. The data analysts who used to work in the back of the garages are now comfortably installed alongside the engineers in one of these units. This not only makes for better

communication, it also frees up valuable space in the garage. It is also the venue for the driver-engineer briefings. On the ground floor of the engineers' truck, around a dozen mechanics have room to work on gearboxes, hydraulics and other mechanical components. In the parts truck, the lower level is kitted out as a workshop for minor mechanical and bodywork repairs.
A small lift is used to transport parts from one level to another. This room is set aside for radio maintenance and the unit which works on weather forecasting.
The satellite dishes and antennae are fitted to the roof by a mechanic wearing a safety harness. Nothing is left to chance at McLaren. ■

BAR truck.

Honda truck.

Jordan truck.

Toyota truck.

A Sauber is unloaded from a truck which can transport three cars.

Minardi truck.

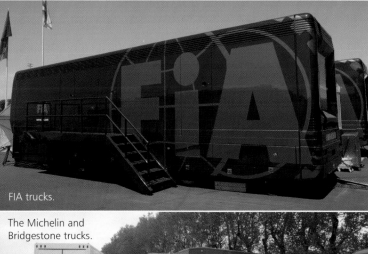

FIA trucks.

The Michelin and Bridgestone trucks.

A stroll
past
the motorhomes

Bernie Ecclestone's motorhome.

The Ferrari motorhome comes together piece by piece.

SCUDERIA FERRARI MARLBORO

SCUDERIA FERRARI

The amount of space they can take up is now rigorously controlled and so making the best use of the space available has become an art. The space is marked out on the tarmac. Paquale Lattuneddu and his assistants enforce the law. There is a war of keeping up with the Jones' played out between the teams, as they all try and out-do one another with ever more luxurious motorhomes. The war is played out in millions of dollars with prestige the prize. The paddock is now the height of luxury, calm and style. Of course one of the purposes of these vehicles is to impress potential new sponsors. McLaren boss Ron Dennis is a true

obsessive when it comes to seeking the ultimate refinement. He was responsible for kicking off the latest round of the motorhome wars, when, in 1998, two gigantic silver grey metallic vehicles turned up in the Imola paddock. They were both fitted with hydraulic lifts which turned them into a double-decker with a joint awning. The price per unit was reckoned to be in the region of one million dollars and in an instant, every other vehicle looked out of date. The McLaren structure insolently dominated the paddock and on the track, their cars were unbeatable. The team boss could walk his head held high, almost as high as his motorhomes.

After the first two rounds outside Europe in 1999, there was an other major surprise when the circus came to Imola for the first European round. The new British American Racing team, run by Craig Pollock, proved it planned to mix it with the big boys. While its cars were not exactly setting the tracks alight, the BAR motorhome certainly caught everyone's attention in the paddock. It took the double decker theme started by McLaren and went a step further. Bernie Ecclestone was not keen on this escalation of the hospitality units and denied the second BAR motorhome access to the paddock.

The McLaren "palace."

The motorhomes are clinically clean.

A big crowd turns out to view the new
McLaren motorhome.

This giant structure took three days and
around ten people to set up. Benetton then
came up with its own unique take on the
theme. Two identical motorhomes were linked
by a central structure which serves as the
reception area. The Anglo-Italian team's
hospitality area looked more like a
discotheque.

Ferrari has gone for the classic approach with
luxuriously appointed vehicles. In 2000, yet
again at Imola, it was Williams and its engine
partner BMW who moved things along a
notch, with each of them boasting identical
looking motorhomes with adjoining glass
verandas.

At Silverstone, it was Jaguar's turn to unveil
its latest hospitality facility in the rain and
mud which prevailed that year. It took a leaf
out of Benetton's book with a glass and
metal central atrium slung between two
vehicles, which looks particularly impressive at
night. A huge chrome jaguar cat was placed
over the entrance, but Ecclestone was not

Feeding time.

impressed. "The paddock is not a zoo. Maybe we could have a prancing horse at Ferrari and a lion at Peugeot." A fortnight later in Barcelona, the chrome cat had been left at home.

Let's take a look at this structure in more detail. The two units are 13.5 metres in length. The structure took 14 weeks to build, the work undertaken by a company in York. The central atrium has a wooden parquet floor and can accommodate 40 guests at meal times and ten more in each of the two fixed units. A bar and reception area feature on a lower level to the atrium. The kitchen is hidden behind screens at the back. The whole unit sits a metre above the ground and of course it is air conditioned. The side units are used as offices, kitted out with all the latest technology, with several phone lines, televisions, satellite links, computers and Internet access. The unit takes ten people three days to put up and the jaguar which made that single appearance was four metres in length and weighed just forty kilos. The design and decoration was conceived by Jaguar Racing and it took three weeks to apply the metallic green paint. Two 38 tonne trailer units carry all the equipment and the total cost is estimated at around 4 million Euro. The Williams structure certainly caught

The BMW-Williams personnel use these C1 scooters.

The tables are laid at BMW, awaiting the guests.

people's attention and Ian Fraser, who built it has now received several orders for similar projects. This new generation of motorhome is designed to have a life of around ten years, but the manufacturer thinks the customer will probably want something new after just five years!

Ron Dennis' old motorhomes are now doing sterling work for the Jordan team. When Paul Stoddart brought the Minardi team back from the brink, he replaced the Faenza squad's old-fashioned motorhomes with two units acquired from the Sultan of Brunei. The Williams structure is far more straightforward than those units used by Jaguar and BAR. A conventional motorhome costs in the region of one million Euro.

The Sauber motorhome.

Today there are thirty motorhomes in the paddock, all neatly parked within strict parameters. A motorhome can cover an area no greater than 14 by 5.5 metres including the awning. There is no height restriction, except that suppliers such as Bridgestone, Michelin and Honda are not allowed double deckers. A gap of 50 centimetres separates the vehicles and Jaguar and Benetton were the first to exploit this loophole to join two units together, making use of the extra gap to provide a bigger area to welcome guests. In 2002, McLaren and Mercedes, who were entitled to three motorhomes, produced one structure to fill this allocated space.

The Communications Centre therefore gained an extra metre, which is a significant increase. It covers an area of 14 square metres, based on the dimensions of three individual units and the two 50 centimetre gaps, with a length of 17.5 metres. The ground floor consists of a central dining area, with driver rest rooms and offices on either side, further offices on the upper level, along with two terraces providing views over the entire paddock.

On the technical front, the FIA and the teams are reaching agreement on rules to cut costs in the sport, such as the introduction of a regulation insisting that the F1 cars use only one engine during the course of a race weekend. However, Ron Dennis appears to have taken a different view, while the word economy is on everyone's lips, he and his partner Mercedes allowed themselves to introduce a hospitality unit which makes every other team's look out of date. It is a grandiose folly. A steel, aluuminium and glass structure, it resembles a medieval fortress, while the team kit worn by the staff looks as though it has stepped off the set of a science fiction film. It is beautifully finished in shades of black and grey evoking a Star

The Jordan motorhome.

Welcome to the world of BAR: the interior is painted in the colours of the title sponsor, it features sliding doors, a spiral staircase, carbon toilets and a kitchen.

Wars feel and it would be a perfect location for a big studio production. As night falls, its lights dazzle the paddock and the arrival of a space ship populated by little green men on its terrace would not be out of place. Erecting the structure begins on the Sunday before the grand prix. Six trailer units disgorge six cubes which make up the basis of the construction and one of the trucks is equipped with a crane to lower them into position. It takes a further two days to finish the job. The handbook reckons on fifteen hours work for ten people. The first time it was built up, eighteen staff took three days of hard work to do it. It takes a further two days to dismantle.

A smiling Ron Dennis has always refused to reveal the name of the architect. "He is my personal architect. I will not tell you his name, because other teams will soon be copying us." Of course, the cost of the project has also remained a secret. There is talk of ten million Euros and a two year design time. The rooms and offices all bear the names of

circuits such as Silverstone and Hockenheim on the ground floor. This is where the press offices are located along with a large driver rest area. The kitchens, bars and small meeting rooms all bear the mark of McLaren. It might smack of megalomania but no one is indifferent to its appearance. On the Thursday of the San Marino Grand Prix, Dennis launched his new creation to the F1 media, standing at the top of one of its two spiral staircases, looking down on a packed atrium, where he made it clear the press were more than welcome. It certainly signalled a change in attitude towards the media from this team, which had never appeared so open or generous, even offering snack packs for the press when they have to work late into the night on Sunday after a race. It was a new breakthrough in the world of the motorhome. Of course, there were suggestions that the money would have been better spent on improving the team's on-track performance, but at the end of the day, a little eccentricity does not go amiss in Formula 1. ∎

Stage by stage, the Renault motorhome takes shape.

The stairs are erected.

The sliding doors are in place.

The Jaguar motorhome.

One of the meeting rooms in the Jaguar motorhome.

The Minardi motorhome.

The Toyota motorhome.

Private motorhomes belonging to David Coulthard, Jenson Button and Jacques Villeneuve.

37

The Private Sector

In 2003, there are 31 motorhomes in the paddock.

- 4 Ferrari (1 team, 1 media, 1 sponsor guests, 1 Vodafone)
- 1 McLaren Communications Centre (team, drivers, guests)
- 2 Jordan (1 team management, 1 drivers and guests)
- 1 Jaguar (two units joined together)
- 1 Jaguar (drivers and team)
- 1 Williams (made of two units for the team and for BMW)
- 1 HP (Williams sponsor)
- 1 Renault (two units joined together)
- 1 Renault
- 2 Sauber (guests and team)
- 1 BAR (two units joined together)
- 2 Minardi (two two storey units)
- 1 Toyota (two units joined together)
- 1 Honda
- 1 Bridgestone
- 1 Michelin
- 1 Karl-Heinz Zimmerman, for Bernie Ecclestone and VIP guests
- 1 Bernie Ecclestone (office)

Jean Todt

Flavio Briatore

David Richards

Eddie Jordan

Peter Sauber

In the paddock, all the team bosses and Bernie Ecclestone agreed to allow a glimpse into their offices. Behind the tinted windows is where all the deals are discussed.

Frank Wiiliams

Ron Dennis

Tony Purnell

Ove Anderson

Paul Stoddart

Bernie Ecclestone

Running a motorhome

(with Vincent CROVISIER)

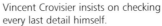

Vincent Crovisier insists on checking every last detail himself.

Born on 25th July 1967 at Toulon, Vincent Crovisier is the man in charge of the Michelin motorhome. "I studied hotel management, then business and graphic arts. At the same time, I was keen on karting and helped out with my two younger twin brothers who raced."

In 1985, he met Olivier Panis at a kart race and followed him to Formula Renault and F3. "We didn't have a bean and camped at the tracks. They were carefree days with no concern about what the next day would bring. I was 18 and working for nothing on the cars and was Olivier's general dogsbody."

Things got serious when Olivier started in Formula 1 in 1994 and he ended up running the Ligier motorhome the following year, but it did not last long. Then, in 1997, Alain Prost bought Ligier and a new deal was done. "I stayed four years with Prost. At the end of 2000, I got a contract with Michelin. It was an evolution for me with a higher level of responsibility. I had to start from scratch, recruiting the personnel and I was given carte blanche. I wanted to offer something a bit better than the usual paddock plate of pasta and I was equally determined to offer a very warm welcome."

In 2001, Crovisier spent 246 days away from home. "I often drive the motorhome myself. I don't have to, but I like being involved with everything. I buy the bare minimum on site, bringing nearly everything from France in a refrigerated truck. I choose the suppliers carefully to be sure of good quality. I use a lot of regional produce with cheeses coming straight from the farm."

Michelin also organises special events, like an Auvergne evening at the French GP and a chocolate soiree in Austria. "It adds some fun to the paddock." During a grand prix, around a hundred people eat at the Michelin motorhome, including forty team members. "We are always striving for perfection." ∎

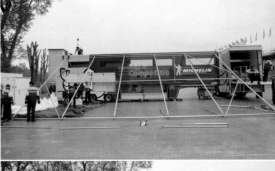

Stephane Laurens, Nacera and Sylvain Scotti present the chocolate evening.

(with Paul EDWARDS)

A trained chef, Paul Edwards worked in restaurants in Barbados and the West Indies in the Seventies and Eighties. "After that, I moved back to Europe and decided to set up my own restaurant in Kensington in London. A decade later, Jackie Stewart suggested I do the catering for his F3000 motorhome. That was in 1991." Three years later, Frank Williams made him an offer to work for his team and so Paul Edwards landed in F1.

"I have happy memories of those days. I started when Ayrton Senna did." Paul Edwards' reputation spread like wildfire through the paddock. Jordan and new arrivals Bridgestone used his services and he set up Edwards Hospitality. His work now extends far beyond catering. He is responsible for all the logistics and organisation for his clients' motorhomes. These require discipline to erect and dismantle. When British American Racing started in F1, it called on Paul Edwards.

The Williams team was sponsored by a rival tobacco brand, so Frank let him go. "So we lost Williams when BAR came along. But we still look after Williams at test sessions. Today, we have contracts with BAR, Jordan and Bridgestone in F1. We also look after Jacques Villeneuve's and Jenson Button's personal motorhomes. In motorbikes, we look after the Fogarty team and the Prodrive Ferrari in GT racing."

Edwards Hospitality employs fifty five people at each race and Edwards is proud to point out that includes two chefs stolen from Ferrari! At each Grand Prix there are also four English chefs. In his fifties and always an F1 fan, he still has a soft spot for Barbados and so he recently bought a hotel there. "It's a new adventure." ■

In the kitchen

(with **Stephane LAURENS**)

working at the circuits with Elf in 1996 as the French fuel company became one of the most popular watering holes in the paddock and there would often be a fight to get a seat at lunchtime.

In 1997, he tried a brief switch to Prost and then Bridgestone. But unhappy with the constraints placed upon him he left the paddock in '99, only to return a few months later with Peugeot. When Peugeot pulled out of F1, he was left without a job, but not for long as he soon found a berth at Michelin in 2001. He was also working on rallies for the Citroen team, but these days he has cut down the travelling, preferring to concentrate on F1.

"We do all we can to satisfy our clientele. Their satisfaction is our goal. I like to experiment with our meals, trying something new, doing interesting things with vegetables, finding the best wines to go with the dishes we create. Recently, we have also included a

buffet service so people can help themselves." Given that Michelin is famous for its red guides, listing and rating restaurants in various countries, it is evident that the Michelin motorhome has to maintain an incredibly high standard of cuisine and there is little doubt that it has succeeded. That is quite an achievement given the constraints of working in a vehicle rather than in a restaurant proper. ■

The Michelin motorhome chef is naturally a Frenchman. Stephane Laurens was born on 22nd February 1972 in Albi. After catering studies he worked in one of the best restaurants in France. A lifelong Formula 1 fan, he began

Karl-Heinz with Bernie Ecclestone.

(with Karl-Heinz ZIMMERMANN)

At the races staged in Europe it was quite common for the paddock to be deafened by the noise of a cannon being fired. No one took much notice: it was just Karl-Heinz Zimmerman on top of his motorhome, firing off a salvo in honour of one of his guests. The Zimmermann motorhome is a popular venue for celebrating race wins. After the events of September 11th 2001, he was forced to leave it at home in Austria because of problems with customs.

Karl-Heinz Zimmermann runs a charming hotel near the ski runs of Lech in the Tyrol. The "Gasthaus Alpenblick" is famous in the area. As a summer sideline, Zimmermann runs the motorhome where Bernie Ecclestone entertains his guests.

"At the end of the 60s, I knew Jochen Rindt and his brother very well. Walter Wolf, former F1 team owner, Niki Lauda and Nelson Piquet all stayed in my hotel and one day they invited me to the 1978 Canadian Grand Prix. Then I started coming to other races. In 1987, at Monza, I had brought along some foie gras, caviar and home made marinated salmon at a time when all you could get in the paddock were some sad sandwiches. Then Camel boss Duncan Lee suggested I come and run his motorhome. I knew Lotus boss Peter Warr very well and I was not sure if it was a good idea to work for a friend. But I accepted and started in 1988, looking after the Lotus motorhome and then the Camel one up to the end of 1993."

Running his alpine activities in the winter, Zimmermann would move over to Formula 1 at the first sign of spring. When Camel pulled out, he switched to running the Rothmans then Winfield facilities for the Williams team. When the cigarette company pulled out at the end of 1999, Ecclestone asked him to take over looking after his guests.

Prof Watkins, Niki Lauda and Norbert Haug are also regular visitors, as are the Schumacher brothers. After a win, they turn up to relax in the most secret and discrete motorhome in the paddock. Far from prying eyes, the drivers have been known to enjoy a beer or two and even a cigar.

And the cannon? "It was given to me by a friend, so I brought it along and to celebrate a win one Sunday night I took it up to the roof and fired it. We all laughed and the paddock shook. A tradition was born."

Zimmermann's reputation for fine food and a warm welcome spread through the paddock. He now has a staff of 25 at each grand prix. Apart from the Bernie motorhome, he also looks after the Toyota facility. "Every year, when the skiing season is over, I can't wait to get back to the special world of Formula 1, where I have a lot of friends. Then, I am glad to get back to the mountains after the final race in Japan. No way, could I run both businesses at the same time." ∎

Karl-Heinz with his friend, Niki Lauda.

The FormulaOne PaddockClub the base for Allsport management

The kingdom of the Formula One Paddock Club. The place to see and be seen at all the Formula 1 Grands Prix.

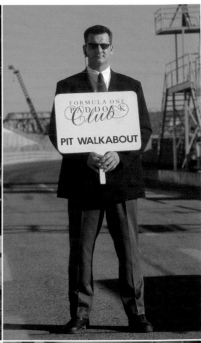

The Austrian Paddock Club.

The kingdom of the Formula One Paddock Club is the place to see and be seen at all the Formula 1 Grands Prix. It is the most civilised way to spend time at every race on the F1 calendar. Its origins go back to a request from Bernie Ecclestone to Patrick McNally to set up a Paddock Club at the 1984 French Grand Prix at Dijon, a race won by Niki Lauda. It was the first time in the sport's history that the decision makers and movers and shakers could gather together in an exclusive atmosphere to enjoy the best hospitality, while networking on a professional and friendly level. It provides an opportunity to discover the world of Formula 1 in a very personalised and high class fashion.

Everything is of the highest standard; the welcome, the service, the catering and the generally relaxed atmosphere. The Paddock Club's first guests got to see everything to do with the sport. They were at the heart of the action, missing out on nothing, thanks to a television link to the hospitality areas.

The Formula One Paddock Club is the most sophisticated form of corporate entertainment on offer at any of the world's big sporting events, such as Roland Garros, Wimbledon, the World Cup, the Tour de France and the start of international yachting races.

As the first of its kind, the Formula One Paddock Club is constantly looking for ways to improve and to diversify in terms of its service, catering, wine list and the elegant smiles of its hostesses.

The idea has met with universal success, breaking down any cultural or language barriers from Suzuka to Silverstone, from Hockenheim to Monza. The facility is located as near to the paddock and the race track as possible. Usually, it is situated above the pits, affording a great view of the start and finish of the Grand Prix. It also gives guests a unique view of the action down below in the pit lane as the mechanics and engineers work on the cars. Over the years, its organisation has become ever more professional and has

The Sepang Paddock Club in Malaysia.

The Williams VIP Paddock Club.

turned into a genuine five star operation, which travels the world offering the best of everything.

It is regarded as a highly practical conduit for business to business discussions amongst the various sponsors and team guests. It provides the Formula 1 teams and their partners with a useful communications tool as they can invite whosoever they see fit. Being invited is in itself an honour. The Paddock Club continues to increase in size and stature year by year and tickets now have to be bought at least one year in advance.

Each ticket includes general access to the circuit and guests can then enjoy everything on offer in the club including any shows, a

bar and even a massage facility. Guests have their own reserved parking area from where they are transported to the Paddock Club. Each team or sponsor which buys into a Paddock Club unit can dress it as it sees fit, with its own décor to personalise it in whatever way it deems suitable.

The Paddock Club welcomes guests from across the social strata; from presidents of multi-nationals to employees who are being rewarded for their efforts. It has now become a key marketing tool. The Paddock Club provides an identical service at each grand prix with the same staff operating it at all the races, providing the highest standards of

cuisine and wine. The same company travels the globe to ensure the highest standards and the Club also provides its own security service.

A visit to the Paddock Club has become a must for the great and the good, while Formula 1 has proved its worth as one of the best means of communication available in the international sports arena. Several billion television viewers watch each grand prix live, but only a few can experience the luxury of the Paddock Club over a grand prix weekend and this exclusivity is its trump card. The majority of guests can only dream of a second visit, which ensures its continued success.

Paddy McNally and Bernie Ecclestone visit the new TAG-Heuer shop.

In Barcelona, as at many circuits, the Paddock Club is located above the pits.

A look at the pits in Magny-Cours.

THE FORMULA ONE PADDOCK CLUB FACTS AND FIGURES

The club's structure above the pits and the tents and flooring for the village are erected ten to fifteen days before an event.

Most of the work is carried out from the Monday to the Thursday prior to the race.

Around twenty trucks transport all the structure and equipment from one grand prix to the next, carrying a total of around 880 tonnes of equipment.

A daily timetable is laid out for suppliers to organise the distribution of supplies in a clear and logical fashion.

Here are some figures for a Grand Prix:
- Fifty chefs and ten patissier chefs.
- 7 electricians.
- Security: around 20 guards (some trained as bodyguards) 24 hours a day.
- Decoration: 7 specialist florists and floral arrangers.
- Cleaning: 20 permanent staff.
- Toilets: ultra modern high level facility.
- Audiovisual: 3 staff to install the flat screens and ensure picture feed throughout the weekend.
- Electronic access gate: 3 permanent staff
A maintenance and support crew
Twenty hostesses.
- In 3 days the facility gets through around 30 cubic metres of water (toilets, kitchen, etc.)
- 7500 sq. metres of carpet and 8000 sq.

metres of awning.
- 16 kilometres of electrical cabling, weighing 25 tonnes.
- guests drink 5000 litres of orange juice.
- 10,000 cut flowers are on display.
- 6 tonnes of cutlery and 30,000 plates.

At each Grand Prix, the Formula One Paddock Club employs 500 staff

Cost of access to Formula One Paddock Club (except the Australian and Brazilian Grands Prix, which have their own tariffs.)
Costs are higher for the races outside Europe (Malaysia, Canada, United States and Japan)
All European races charge the same.
Costs vary depending on whether or not guests are invited by a team or as individuals.The cost varies between 2650 and 4200 Euro. ∎

Suzuka (on left) and Hockenheim (above,) the smallest and the biggest Paddock Clubs.

The Magny-Cours Paddock Club.

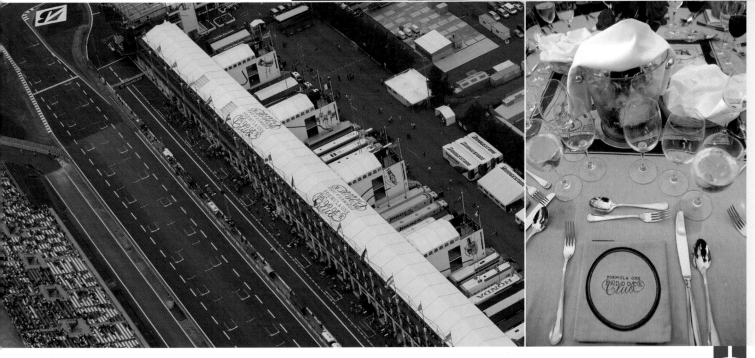

2 PADDOCK LIFE

F1 PADDOCK

chapter 2

2

PADDOCK LIFE

Fortunately, the Formula 1 workers are not the only people to inhabit the paddock. Glamour is now an integral part of the Grand Prix world as the sport is not confined to the back pages of newspapers. People from the world of showbiz, politics and the biggest names from other sports are regular visitors to the pits and the grids. There are also other elements which are now integral to Formula 1.

Paddock access pass

Stickers allowing vehicle access to the centre of the circuit.

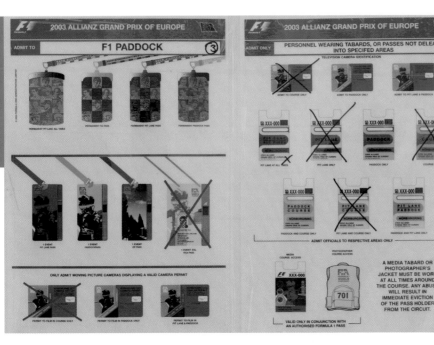

The arrival of the swipe card system at the paddock gates has been a controversial subject. It means everyone's movements are now recorded. Any illegal use is instantly signalled by a red light and an alarm sounding. As Formula 1 grew in popularity, so the paddock was the regarded as the promised land for the fans.

In the past, one pass was enough to get several people into the paddock, by the simple expedient of slipping a pass back through the fence. This meant the paddock ended up bursting at the seams, with drivers constantly pursued for autographs and photos. A limit on the number of guest passes had made this method the norm and the paddock was stifling under the load. One could deplore this attitude and claim the paddock is now a no man's land. Twenty years ago, one could buy a ticket to the Paul Ricard paddock for the French Grand Prix for 15 Euro. At Silverstone, just a few moveable barriers separated the F1 enclosure from the general public and only typical English reserve overcame the fans' desire to get closer to the action. It would never have worked at Monza, where the fans would climb high walls with barbed wire to get in.

Over a period of time, security guards were employed, high fences erected and plastic sheeting was put up to keep the F1 world hidden from prying eyes. Only electrified fencing seems to be missing! The public takes a very dim view of these rules. But without wishing to appear selfish, one has to admit it makes life easier for the media as they have easier access to the drivers.

Up until a few years ago, access to the Monaco paddock was free at certain times of the day. The fans laid siege to the team motorhomes and the drivers disappeared from sight. Today, many reckon the paddock atmosphere is soulless and clinical. Perhaps the system used in American races is the one to adopt to please the fans. There, long autograph sessions are organised every day which give fans a chance to meet the drivers. None of the drivers fail to turn up.
In 2000 at Silverstone, the organisers had cut windows with small counters in the paddock fencing near the exit. This meant drivers could sign autographs in safety and for a large number of fans. The following year, these windows had vanished. Why? Were the fans too noisy? ■

Paddock Club pass

VIP pass

Permanent Pit lane pass   Permanent Paddock pass

Fernando Alonso's permanent pass.   VIP pass

Paddock entrances

Melbourne 2000

F1 PADDOCK

Melbourne 1999

Melbourne 2003

FORMULA ONE PADDOCK

Monza 2000

Formula One Paddock

Kuala Lumpur 2003

Melbourne 2003

THE WORLD ACCORDING TO FORMULA ONE

Kuala Lumpur 2002

FORMULA 1 PADDOCK

SEE YOU SOON

Circuit main entrance

Rubens Barrichello drives his Ferrari into the Imola circuit.

David Coulthard and his hand luggage.

Rubens Barrichello tackles a signing session.

Michael Schumacher and Jean Todt arrive in a Lancia.

Michael and Corinna Schumacher arrive at the Imola circuit by Maserati.

Michael Schumacher's arrival often prompts the odd mini-riot.

Jacques Villeneuve and his PA prefer to travel by scooter.

Michael and Corinna by scooter.

Justin Wilson and his MG.

Mark Webber arrives in the very latest Land Rover product.

Jarno
Trulli

The Boss' parking slot for Bernie Ecclestone and his luxurious Maybach.

This is the BMW X5 4x4 which Juan Pablo was driving when he was caught by a speed-camera doing 204 km/h on the A8 motorway in France.

Juan Pablo Montoya with his wife, Connie.

A relaxed arrival for Fernando Alonso.

The Organisation of a Grand Prix

At the 2001 German Grand Prix, the FIA allowed the French magazine Auto Hebdo to penetrate the nerve centre of a grand prix's organisation. Here are the photos from that visit....

Photos 1: On the Thursday prior to each grand prix, at the end of the morning, Race Director Charlie Whiting, accompanied by colleague Herbie Blash, carries out a scrupulous track inspection, corner by corner. He checks all key areas such as the tyre walls and their anchorage points, the gravel traps and the condition of the track.

Photo 2: After this inspection, which can last several hours, he meets the drivers, here with Michael Schumacher, president of the GPDA (Grand Prix Drivers Association) to discuss possible improvements to safety measures.

Photo 3: In the half light of race control, situated on the second floor of the control tower, Charlie Whiting, the FIA officials, the stewards and the race organisers keep a close watch on forty screens which cover all key areas on the circuit. No offence can escape the eye of these eighteen observers. The whole feeling of this room is akin to the control centre for a space mission. All decisions as to whether a practice session or the race should be stopped emanate from this nerve centre.

Photos 4 and 5: At one end of pit lane, a garage is given over to scrutineering. During qualifying, a team of scrutineers led by Jo Bauer, assisted by Michel Lepraist checks cars at random. The cars are pushed onto weighing scales, where all the various measurements to which the car must conform are checked. The level surface allows

5 6

all these checks to be carried out in a matter of seconds. Once on the scales, a team of six scrutineers control various heights and other measurements; all completed within two minutes before the cars are released back to the teams, so that a minimum amount of track time is lost. Jo Bauer controls the procedure from behind his desk. At the end of the race, all finishers undergo this technical inspection. The race result is only declared as official, once the procedure has been completed.

Photo 6: At the end of qualifying, the drivers kept in parc ferme are weighed with their crash helmets. Here we see Juan Pablo

Montoya, the latter having just taken pole position. After the race, all drivers who finish go through the same procedure. After this session, Jo Bauer gets to leave his control post to examine other points in detail, along with Michel Lepraist.

Photos 7 and 8: In parc ferme, Peter Tibbets takes fuel samples from a Williams. Then, in the FIA laboratory truck, it is examined to ensure it conforms to the regulations.

Photo 9: After this session and the end of the race, in another section of the FIA truck, Claudio Garavine checks the data from the cars' black boxes. ∎

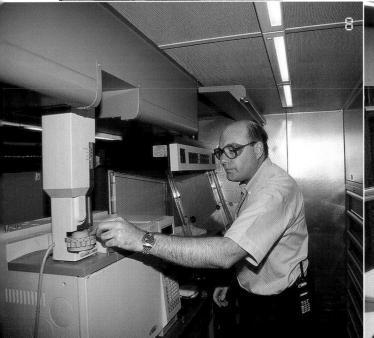

8 9

The **Driver's** **parade**

Every race day, in the late morning, after the pre-race briefing, the drivers do a lap of the track to wave at their fans.

A red carpet is a must for the drivers.

Kuala Lumpur 2003.

Schumi is running late for the 2001 Malaysian Grand Prix parade.

A flat bed truck is usually the vehicle of choice for the drivers to parade in front of their fans. This traditional part of the weekend, normally takes place on Sunday morning at 11h15.

At the French Grand Prix, the drivers' parade makes use of prestige machinery. Here we see Coulthard and Häkkinen in a Bugatti.

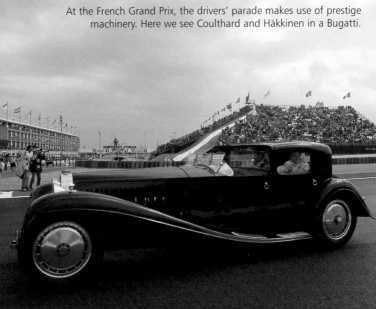

Monza 2000.

Felipe Massa waves to his fans.

F1 **Girls**

No one is immune to their charms, as they bring a touch of glamour to the paddock.

Stars
Cinema...

Formula 1 is ever more popular in the media. Personalities are drawn to the world of Grand Prix racing. Here is the exclusive Visitors Book from the paddock over the past few years.

Sean Connery

Alain Delon

Michael Douglas

Paul Newman

Jackie Stewart

Rowan Atkinson

Jackie Stewart

Rubens Barrichello

Arnold Schwarzenegger

Elizabeth Hurley

Jean Alesi

Hugh Grant

Wesley Snipes

Mark Webber

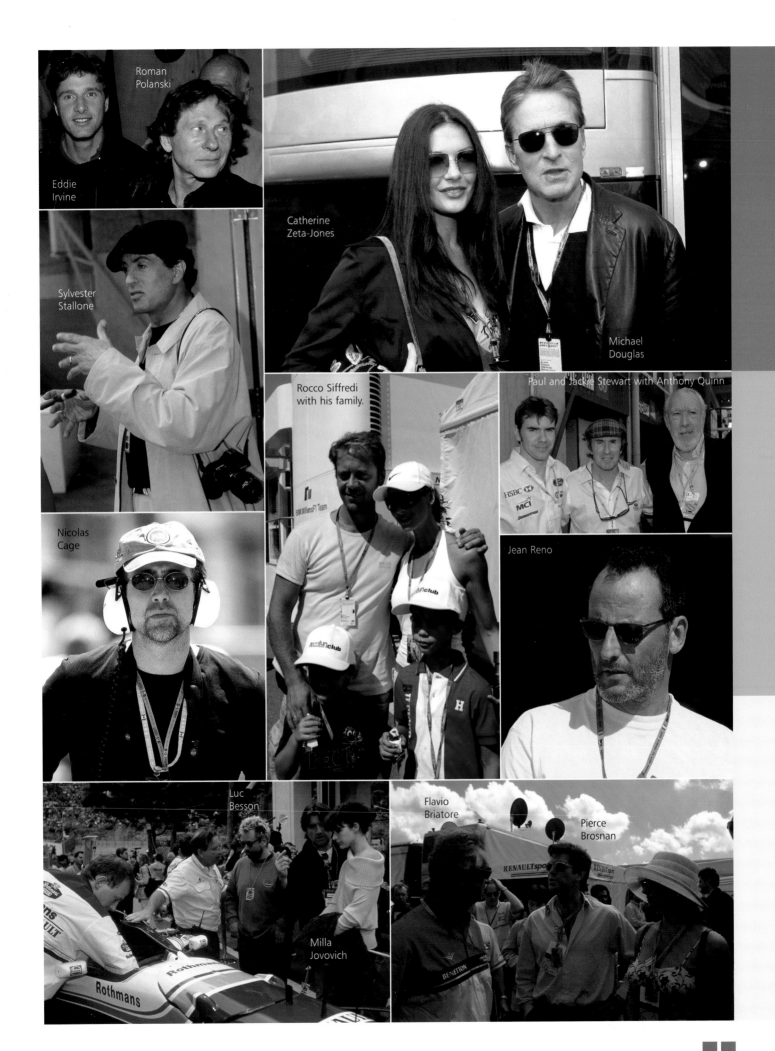

Roman Polanski

Eddie Irvine

Catherine Zeta-Jones

Michael Douglas

Sylvester Stallone

Rocco Siffredi with his family.

Paul and Jackie Stewart with Anthony Quinn

Nicolas Cage

Jean Reno

Luc Besson

Flavio Briatore

Pierce Brosnan

Milla Jovovich

Stars Sports

Edwin Moses

Alessandro Di Pietro

Jean Alesi

Zinedine Zidane

Eric Cantona

Boris Becker

Norbert Haug

David Ginola

Alain Delon
AlbertoTomba

Diego Maradona

Michael Schumacher

Ronaldo

Alex Barros, Katja Poensgen et Loris Capirossi

Shaquile O'Neal

Eddie Irvine

Juan Pablo Montoya

Arantxa Sanchez

Luc Alphand

Jean Alesi

Carl Lewis

Jan Ullrich

Michael Johnson

Merlene Ottey

Stars Music

Eddie Jordan   Chris Rea

Kylie Minogue

Erja and Mika
Häkkinen

Andrea
Boccelli

Mick Jagger

Bernie
Ecclestone

Bono (U2)

The late and great
George Harrison

Deep Purple with Eddie Jordan.

Phil Collins

Cher

Danii Minogue

Liberty X

Ozzy Osbourne

Chris De Burgh

Mick Hucknall (Simply Red).

Eros Ramazotti

...Brian Adams

Kim Wilde

Nigel Mansell

Jarno Trulli and...

Drivers'
Wives

Corinna and Michael Schumacher.

Connie and Juan Pablo
Montoya.

Simone Adbelnour and David Coulthard.

Silvana and Rubens Barrichello

Jenson Button and Louise.

Nick Heidfeld and Patricia.

Jarno Trulli and his girlfriend.

Cristiano Da Matta and his girlfriend

Justin Wilson and his girlfriend

Giancarlo and Luna Fisichella.

Kimi Räikkönen with Jenni Dahlman.

Tanja and Heinz-Harald Frentzen.

Felipe Massa and his girlfriend.

Ralf and Cora
Schumacher.

Jacques Villeneuve and Ellie Green.

Olivier and Anne Panis.

Drivers' homes in Monaco

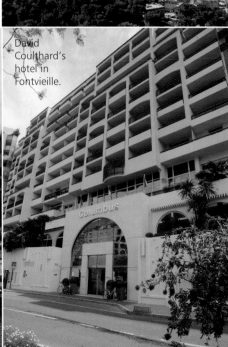

The Fontvieille port in Monaco.

David Coulthard's hotel in Fontvieille.

Ralf Schumacher's yacht.

David Coulthard's apartment at Rafael-Fontvieille.

Juan Pablo Montoya's yacht.

The Emilie Palace is home to Juan Pablo Montoya.

Jenson Button's yacht.

The Sea Side Plaza is home to Heinz-Harald Frentzen.

Giancarlo Fisichella on board his yacht.

Cristiano Da Matta lives in the Edenstar in Fontvieille.

Jacques Villeneuve's yacht.

Ayrton Senna used to live in this apartment in Fontvieille.

Olivier Panis on his yacht.

Hotels and restaurants

The Dorint Hotel is right by the Nürburgring circuit.

The paddock and the people who live there over the weekend is like one big family. This heart of the Formula 1 world only really comes to life on the Thursday prior to a race when team members and the media arrive. For several years now, team personnel all travel in a smart uniform with suits and ties, as elegance is everything in F1. Once in the paddock, the workers change into team uniform. When everyone is ready for work, invariably the question, "which hotel are you in" dominates the conversation.

We have drawn up a list, not a comprehensive one, of the best hotels in the vicinity of the tracks, which all the top teams fight over. Very often, the top hotels insist on a five night minimum stay, even though many F1 folk are only there for three nights. These

Fossati restaurant at Monza.

rooms can cost an average of 400 Euro per night, although Monaco can prove much more expensive.

If you fancying visiting a grand prix and living in luxury, with the chance of bumping into the drivers at breakfast or in the lifts, here are some details of the hotels favoured by the world of Formula 1.

Australia
Melbourne: Crown Plazza, Méridien At Rialto, The Windsor.
Malaysia
Kuala Lumpur Airport: Panpacific.
Kuala Lumpur: Palace of the Golden Horses, The Mandarin.
Brazil
Sao Paolo: Transamerica, Caesar Park, Sheraton.
San Marino
Imola: Olimpia, Grand Hotel Donatello, Hotel Molino Rosso.
Dozza: Monte del Re.
Spain
Barcelone: Ritz, Rey Juan Carlos I.

Monaco
Monte Carlo: Hôtel de Paris, Hôtel Hermitage, Monte-Carlo Grand Hôtel, Méridien Beach Plaza, Monte Carlo Beach Hôtel, Mirabeau.
Canada
Montreal: Loews Le Vogue, La Montagne, Le Delta, Le Grand, Queen Elizabeth.
Europe
Nürburgring: Hotel Dörint Motodrom.
France
Magny-Cours: Holiday Inn, La Renaissance.
Varennes-Vauzelles: Château de la Rocherie.
Great Britain
Silverstone: Wittlebery Hotel, Golf Course Circuit Hotel.
Northampton: The Northampton Moat House
Milton Keynes: Forte Crest Hotel.
Germany
Hockenheim: Hotel Motodrom.
Walldorf: Holiday Inn.
Heidelberg: Der Europaïsche Hof.
Hungary
Budapest: Intercontinental, Marriott Budapest, Hilton Budapest, Hyatt Budapest, Hotel Béke Radisson, Gd Hotel Corvinus Kempiski.

Belgium
Francorchamps: Le Roannay.
Spa: Hotel Alfa Balmoral.
Italy
Monza: Hotel de la Ville.
Canonica: Hotel Fossati.
Milano: Grand Hotel, Principe Di Savoia.
Como (by helicopter): Villa d'Este, Castello Di Pomerio.
United States
Indianapolis: Hotel du Circuit, Hilton, Hyatt.
Japan
Suzuka: Suzuka Circuit Hotel.

Having sorted out a hotel, the next question is where to eat. There are some restaurants which are very popular in Formula 1 circles and are almost F1 canteens with the entire paddock turning up. Getting a table can be extremely difficult and reservations are essential.

Popular in Brazil are the Charascaria where all sorts of grilled meats are served on sword-like skewers. Everyone heads for the Fogo de Chao at 964 Avenida Santo Amaro in Sao Paulo. It is a must do. The caipirinha drink, based on sugar cane

El Trabuc restaurant at Granollers near the Barcelona track.

Jacques Villeneuve's restaurant, Newtown in Montreal.

alcohol, has been known to turn the quietest man in the paddock into a very chatty soul indeed!

Italy and Imola is a favourite for lovers of pasta, a dish that is a great staple for all the drivers. In Italy, it is impossible to get a bad plate of pasta. At the circuit entrance is a particular favourite, the Ristorante Naldi. Also popular are Zio and San Domenico. Obviously, Monza and the Italian Grand Prix is also a big hit with pasta lovers. The Canonica Fossati is an institution: ten kilometres from the circuit, this magnificent auberge is a big hit with the drivers.

For the Spanish GP, the El Trabuc restaurant is just a few kilometres from the track on the road to Granollers and is packed with F1 people over race weekend. Raw ham, tomato bread, grilled goat and the famous "Marques de Caceres" red wine are not to be missed. But prices have become prohibitive over the past few years. If you can face the trip into Barcelona, the Ramblas area and its famous seafood platters are worth the journey. Monaco is noted for its Italian restaurants and Polpetta, 2 rue du Paradis is an institution. It was a tradition at the end of the evening to go out in the road and whack

The Circuit Hotel at Suzuka in Japan, with karaoke.

Buca di Beppo restaurant in Indianapolis.

Stars and Bars in Monaco.

champagne corks with a golf club but the neighbours objected and the tradition has ended. Several drivers live in the Fontvieille area and they tend to eat in the many pizzerias, such as the Michelangello and La Saliere. Stars 'n Bars near the paddock is a trendier spot with a rock 'n roll atmosphere, but the drivers dare not turn up during race week in case they cause a riot. The Rascasse restaurant provides the perfect opportunity to lunch within metres of the cars on the track. In Monaco, food is less important than being seen in the right places, but the drivers prefer to keep out of sight at home during race week.

In Montreal, the Montagne restaurant is worth a visit. It is located in the hotel and the street of the same name. Just across the road, you should go and have a drink in Jacques Villeneuve's bar-restaurant-club,

called Newtown. Restaurants in Old Montreal are more typical. A warm welcome is guaranteed everywhere and the quality of the meals is very good.

At Magny-Cours, in the heart of Charolais beef country, good restaurants are plentiful. The hotel-restaurant La Renaissance in the village which gives the circuit its name, is a gastronomic delight. Also worth a visit is La Grande Chaumiere at Saint-Pierre Le Moutiere. Travel further afield and there are plenty of charming restaurants alongside the Loire where one can eat and drink remarkably well, without choking over the bill!

For Hockenheim, one can eat very well in the old city of Heidelberg and the castle is worth a visit. Closer to the track, the Vorfelder and Haus Landgraf restaurants in Waldorf offer

the delights of an outdoor dining area. At the Nürburgring, try the Zum Gemtlichen Ecke at Adenau.

In Indianapolis, if you like Italian food then head for Buca di Beppo for a Sicilian setting which is a bit disconcerting in the middle of the USA!

In Japan, lovers of the local cuisine can make the most of the sushi bars, serving raw fish. If you are not feeling that adventurous then there are Japanese and Chinese restaurants at the circuit. The Italian Campanella restaurant is a big favourite with the paddock people and one needs to reserve a table two or three days in advance. The drivers tend to eat there every night and often have to escape through the kitchen door to avoid the mass of fans waiting outside. ■

Merchandising

Monaco 2000.

Japan
1999

Nürburgring 2003.

Mario Alquati, his wife and Clay Regazzoni
(centre) in the Seventies.

Merchandising is the term applied
to the sale of goods linked to the
teams and drivers. These items
began appearing on the scene in the
Seventies. At the time, these were restricted to
T-shirts, caps and flags, sold by a few
specialists who turned up at the tracks.

In Monza, Mario Alquati who still runs the
famous "Libreria dello Autodromo" at the
circuit did a clever deal with Jackie Stewart to
market his trademark black cap. "In 1970, we
sold 100,000 of them, a huge figure in those
days. Our agreement even extended to Jackie
coming along for an hour to sign the photo
that went with the cap. We also did a Clay
Regazzoni T-shirt and luckily for us the Ferrari
driver won the race. It caused a riot in front

Imola 1992.

Imola 1990.

Spa-Francorchamps 1996.

of the shop. But merchandising really took off in 1975 with the arrival of tobacco sponsorship and the T-shirt was the top item. We also sold a lot of posters. Then came jackets and other clothes in team and driver colours and stickers were also coming into their own. We were operating at a profit margin of around 2000%."

But a lot of stall holders were soon put out of business as the cost of renting a plot at the track rocketed. Based in San Francisco, French couple Liliane and Jacques Carton run a merchandising business all over the United States. At the start of the Nineties, they decided to conquer Europe, after a trial run in

Canada and Australia. "We did all the European races from 1990 to 1993, except Hungary and we went home in between each race. The merchandise all came through France and we then transported it from there to the tracks. We specialised in pin badges depicting the drivers' helmets. They were designed by George Follmer, a former American F1 driver. In Japan, we soon sold out of those for Senna, Prost, Piquet, Mansell and Nakajima. Over there, I think they thought you had to pin the badge to your skin," said Jacques with a smile. "Even the drivers would come and buy them for their friends. We also did a lot of T-shirts. In those days a handshake was all it took to do the

deal and the drivers just wanted a few badges themselves as a royalty. Guys like Alesi and Barrichello trusted us. We did not need their approval or their agents' permission to sell them."

"We used to be charged around 7000 Euro per weekend to set up a stall," recalled Liliane. "Then in 1994 it shot up to an amazing 25,000 Euro. We could not keep up, with huge travel and freight costs and low profit margins on some items, so we threw in the towel." Today, the Cartons restrict their activities to travelling the length and breadth of the US selling at Indycar, endurance and historic sports car

Nürburgring 2000.

Silverstone 2000.

Silverstone 2000.

Indianapolis 2001, after 9/11.

The official shops in the Nürburgring paddock.

In 2002, a CD was produced featuring Ayrton Senna's favourite music.

Floriano Ottaviani (ARS) with Fernando Alonso, Jarno Trulli and Allan McNish.

meets. But each year, they come to Suzuka for the Grand Prix where the costs are lower. Today the vending areas are controlled by Allsport Management and everything is much more organised than in the past, when even the drivers and teams were sometimes unaware of the products being sold using their name and never got any commission. Now, hordes of lawyers and inspectors weed out those selling contraband merchandise around the circuits and from other outlets.

The sales units must also be of a suitably high standard to blend in with F1's quality image. With the exception of the streets of Monaco, Suzuka and Indianapolis, the independent sellers have virtually disappeared. Teams and drivers have woken up to the potential of this type of operation and the Internet has speeded up the sales process. Michael Schumacher and his manager Willi Weber lead the way, making the German driver the richest sportsman in the world, with sales of

merchandise contributing a major percentage of his income. Schumacher caps are the biggest selling item, at around 10 Euro each and they generate an income of 1.5 million Euro per year.

One of the biggest enterprises in this field is ARS located in San Remo in Italy, set up in 1983 by Floriano Ottaviani which produces amongst other items, around 100,000 caps per year. ■

Suzuka 2000. Michael Schumacher's little fans are not forgotten.

Imola 2002.

Sao Paulo 2000.

A striking contrast between the official paddock shops and the street vendors at Monaco.

An effigy of Michael Schumacher, as a lamp.

Magny-Cours 2000.

3
THE MEDIA

chapter 3

3

THEMEDIA

Their job is providing information and the journalists, photographers, radio reporters and of course the television crews are the backbone of this process. In the press room one can meet fascinating characters who, in their own way, have contributed something to making Formula 1 as popular as it is today. Their eyewitness accounts constitute a history of the sport, while television is king when it comes to media coverage at the grands prix.

Journalists and photographers

Didier Braillon ("L'Equipe", French daily paper) and Christian Tortora in Mexico in 1981.

Didier Braillon, 20 years later. The job is still more or less the same, but the tools of the trade have changed.

Many journalists and photographers started their careers in Formula 1 thanks to their ability to scale fences. Others, possibly less fit and sporty, used their cunning, their powers of observation and a skill in forgery to produce passes even more authentic than the originals. Some of the journalists and photographers will admit to this crime if pushed.

Up until the mid-Eighties, a bit of nerve and daring saw several pushy types get into the paddock and even the pits without ever being questioned. Until quite recently, one pass was enough to get several people into the paddock, by slipping the pass through the fencing.

But today, a new breed of security man and pass checker has flourished in the paddock.

They are usually recruited for their muscle, their shaven heads and their surly demeanour. The fact they are incapable of thought makes discussion rather difficult.

These days, it is impossible to get into the paddock under false pretences without the precious Open Sesame pass, as rows of electronic control gates now guard every entrance to the promised land that is the paddock.

With the car parks now a long way from the paddock, shuttle buses are used to take the journalists and photographers to the media centre.

With thousands of spectators attending the grands prix, large numbers would love to get closer to their idols. In the past, money would change hands on a regular basis, but that scenario is now inconceivable.

Formula 1 is so fashionable that requests for accreditation are constantly on the increase. For reasons of space, there has to be a limit on how many people are allowed into a media centre and around the circuit. The FIA (Federation Internationale Automobile) controls the distribution of passes and it has been forced to restrict their number.

What is needed to meet the criteria for "Media" accreditation for a Formula 1 Grand Prix?

THE JOURNALISTS

The FIA will only allocate Media accreditation to publications intending to publish a report related to the event for which the accreditation is requested.
A maximum of two representatives

(journalists and/or photographers) per publication may be accredited. Agencies are subject to the same requirements as publications.
Editors of publications are asked kindly to conform to the following principles and procedures in order to ensure that media accreditation is restricted to professional journalists and photographers.

To get a permanent credential for the year: the journalist or the publication must have attended a minimum of 12 rounds during the previous F1 season. The attribution of this credential depends on the decision of a press council which meets to study all the cases. Each pass must carry the bearers photo, along with his name and the name of the publication.

To obtain a pass for an individual event: the publication or journalist must make a request to the FIA at least three weeks prior to the event concerned to the following address:

FIA
Département des relations
extérieures
Service des accréditations
8, Place de la Concorde
75008 PARIS
FRANCE

The FIA considers the Media pass to be a working took and is not to be used for PR, promotional or leisure activities.

The FIA only accredits publications whose quantity and quality meet the FIA criteria and these publications must be on sale to the general public. All electronic media must address their requests to the FOA offices in London.

FIA accredits only the international press according to the country where the event takes place. National press must address its request to the national body, while foreigners make their request through the FIA.

Bernard Cahier, Mike Doodson, Gerard Crombac and Heinz Pruller, the old generation.

THE PHOTOGRAPHERS

To obtain a photographer's pass: Since 1999 the photographers' accreditation in the FIA Formula One World Championship are governed by the following principles.

PERMANENT ACCREDITATION

Press Photographers: In order to qualify for a "press photographer" permanent credential, a publication or agency must supply evidence to have independently covered and published in editorial media matching the FIA's quality and circulation criteria at least 240 pictures of the previous year FIA Formula One World Championship per pass issued, and that his(their) photographer(s) effectively attended a minimum of 12 Formula One events of the previous year Championship.

It must also be proved that:
In case of an agency, the pictures have been regularly sold to publications matching the FIA criteria and have been paid for at the normal commercial rate;
In case of a publication, the pictures published are the original work of the publication's accredited photographer.
Promotional Photographers: Publications or agencies not complying with the above

criteria may be considered "promotional photographers" and obtain a permanent credential by applying to:
Formula One Management Ltd
Promotional Photographers Accreditation
6 Princes Gate - London SW7 -
Great Britain
T (44) 207 584 66 68
F (44) 207 225 02 19

The application must include a file proving professional photographic work and skills. If the application is accepted, the credentials will be submitted to a fee which is intended as a contribution to the promoters of the events for the cost of the photographers' facilities.

RACE-BY-RACE ACCREDITATION - INTERNATIONAL PHOTOGRAPHERS

Press photographers: Publications or agencies applying for single round accreditation must supply evidence of independent coverage of a minimum of 15 pictures per pass issued at each event they have been accredited the previous year, following the same criteria applied for the "permanent accreditation". The number of international "press photographer"

passes will not exceed 30 at each event. Promotional photographers: Accreditation may be obtained following the same principles and procedure set above. The amount of the fee will be the pro-rata.

RACE-BY-RACE ACCREDITATION - NATIONAL PHOTOGRAPHERS

The number of "press photographer" passes issued for the national press will not exceed 12. Other photographers may submit their application as "promotional photographers", following the principles and procedure set above. The amount of the fee will be the pro-rata.

It was not that long ago that the FIA was liberal when it came to handing out passes, while rules were draconian for the Olympic Games or the Football World Cup and other major sporting events. Today, the level of interest generated by Formula 1 means that the FIA has been forced to clamp down on the number of press it accredits.

Official statistics regarding the number of permanent journalists and photographers in the 2002 season:

In Malaysia in 1999, the photographers got together to celebrate the birthday of FIA photographers' representative, Pat Behar,

Journalists Photographers Total

Grand Prix	J	P	Total
Australia	117	73	199
Malaysia	110	68	186
Brasil	94	68	168
San Marino	129	73	210
Spain	133	71	213
Austria	131	73	213
Monaco	136	75	219
Canada	96	63	164
Europe	127	68	203
Great Britain	128	69	205
France	125	70	203
Germany	126	73	207
Hungary	102	72	183
Belgium	119	70	197
Italy	127	71	207
United States	88	59	150
Japan	72	59	137

At the first grand prix of the season, the FIA organises the traditional photo of all the drivers. Independently, the photographers all get to together to photograph all their helmets.

In 2003, 170 publications or agencies were acrredited for all the vents: 138 journalists, 5 photo-journalists, 76 photographers and 3 technicians. 222 permanent credentials were given out in total.

The 170 publications and agencies accredited in 2003:

Great-Britain	32	Finland	3
Germany	27	Greece	3
France	19	Ireland	3
Japan	18	USA	3
Italy	17	Portugal	2
Switzerland	13	South Africa	1
Netherlands	5	Denmark	1
Belgium	5	Rumania	1
Austria	4	Russia	1
Spain	4	Slovénia	1
Brazil	3	Czech Republic	1
Canada	3		

The 76 photographers accredited in 2003 :

Great Britain	21	Spain	3
Germany	12	Greece	2
Japan	11	Netherlands	2
France	10	Austria	1
Italy	5	Denmark	1
Switzerland	3	Finland	1
Belgium	3	Czech Republic	1

Not all the passes carry the same privileges. All permanent pass holders are allowed into pit lane, the paddock and the press room. These passes are distinguished by a red lanyard.

Others, whose pass is hung on a green lanyard are denied access to pit lane. Permanent pass holders are allowed onto the track if they request a special bib to do so, a system set up in 1994. The permanent photographers can chose to wear these individual bibs or a permanent photographer's jacket generously provided by the FIA. 75% of photographers opt for the latter. 150 bibs are produced for each grand prix. They each bear a number so that the identity of the wearer can be tracked down.

All permanent pass holders are allowed access onto the grid. For others, a grid access sticker might be available, in very limited numbers.

In the past there were no rules regarding going trackside, but these days, apart from having the right credentials there are other rules which have to be obeyed. You cannot cross the track less than half an hour before the start of a practice session or the race. A shuttle bus service transports photographers

Buses take journalists and photographers around the circuit.

Today, thanks to the use of portable computers and mobile phones, photographers can send their work to magazines in real time, be it from the press room or at the side of the track.

Media centre for the photographers.

to their vantage points before this deadline. At some tracks, a service road runs parallel to the track and buses can move photographers around during the sessions. Back in the Seventies, you could cross the track in the middle of the session, as long as you had the marshals' permission. But you needed to have good walking legs to get from one end of the circuit to the other, so progress does sometimes have its benefits.

There are also rules regarding pit lane access and while red lanyard holders can walk up and down during practice, it is strictly forbidden during the race because of the inherent danger involved in the pit stops. Another bib allows access to the pit wall. The permanent photographers are divided into five groups, by nationality and language and

The various bibs needed to go out on track and on pit wall.

Media centre for the photographers.

Near or far, nothing escapes the attention of the photographers during the course of a Grand Prix weekend.

each photographer will have this access approximately once per year, the FIA giving out one per group at each race. The major agencies, such as AFP, AP and Reuters have one at each race. Anyone taking pictures from the pit wall is not allowed to cross back again, which means that only four photographers per race get to capture the excitement of the pit stops.

A numbered parking pass for the International Media car park is given out in the media centre to permanent pass holders and is picked up at the preceding race, except for the first race of the season. The car parks are either a short walk from the paddock, or shuttle buses are provided. Teams often beg journalists for any spare passes if they do not have enough for themselves.

A look inside the photographers' room in Barcelona.

In the case of photographers the advent of digital cameras at the end of the Nineties has radically changed working practices. Today, the majority of them spend the afternoon transmitting their photos to a server or to their clients. Depending on the speed of the phone lines, it takes one to two minutes to send one digital photo via computer and the Internet. The downside of this revolutionary technology is the variable quality of the phone lines which can really cause problems during a day's work. Some photographers working for the major agencies actually transmit photos from the side of the track within seconds of shooting them, using a mobile phone to link to the Internet with the computer.

Since 2003, the majority of publications only use digital photos. While the quality is not yet quite up to the level of film, it is only a matter of time. Using digital means that photos no longer have to be scanned and this saves a lot of time. It has resulted in the photographers rooms at the circuits getting ever bigger, as only a few high quality publications insist on still working with film.

A large percentage of the photographers are freelance and covering a whole grand prix season demands a big investment. Travelling Economy Class and sharing hire cars and hotel rooms, the cost per person of a whole season of Formula 1 costs in the region of 20,000 Euro. ■

Keith Sutton and Jad Sherif.

There is an official "Formula One Personnel" car park for the teams and there is also a much smaller area for the drivers and Bernie Ecclestone.

At the welcome desk in the media centre, journalists and photographers reserve their work space on a table plan, while also booking telephone lines. Lockers are also available to leave computers and other equipment. Photographers have the same facility in their work area and photo wiring room.

So how do journalists and photographers go about their business? For events outside Europe, most of them arrive on a Wednesday to recover from jet-lag, while in Europe Thursday is the usual day to turn up in the paddock. Most people turn up in the late morning. Main priority for photographers is a

locker to place all that bulky equipment, while journalists secure a seat in the press office, get a telephone line, sign the attendance register, pick up their parking pass for the next race and then head off into the paddock to look for the latest news stories. Some motorhomes are already up and running on Thursday to greet the ravenous hordes.

The first official press conference of the weekend takes place on Thursday afternoon, allowing journalists working for daily papers to file in the late afternoon or early evening, using e-mail to send their stories. The routine is repeated throughout the weekend and on Sunday night, many journalists do not get away until well past midnight. Others prefer to leave the track and work in the comfort of their hotel room before catching a flight the following morning.

FOPA
Formula
One
Photographer
Association

Alongside all the official bodies operating under the control of FIA and FOA, there is also a group of thirty or so photographers who go by the important sounding title of FOPA, the Formula One Photographers Association. It was established during a particularly liquid dinner at the 1985 German Grand Prix by four English photographers: John Townsend, Steven Tee, Keith Sutton and Crispin Thruston. John Townsend, the chairman of this very British club explains its raison d'etre. "We wanted to create a really informal group, which would also have a serious purpose. It is actually a club for photographers who like to eat and drink well!"

This well rounded epicurean energetically runs this organisation which aims to bring together the best in the profession. FOPA is very international, with its four founding members and an amalgam of Japanese, Italians, Germans, Spaniards, Finns and one honorary Swiss, Jad Sherif.

French photographers were not allowed to be members of this exclusive band. Indeed, shaking hands with a Frenchman could entail blackballing. Then, at the start of the 90s, three Frenchmen, Gilles Levent, Bernard Asset and Jean-Francois Galeron were admitted.

The FOPA emblem is a little pink pig. Annual membership costs £60 and entitles members to a set of four personally monogrammed white polo shirts, featuring the member's national flag and the charming little pig. They are to be worn on each day of a grand prix weekend.

Occasionally, FOPA partners generously dish out gifts such as sweat shirts, jackets and rain coats with the organisation's emblem. As the most important activity is dining, several times a year, various well known sponsors such as Philip Morris, West, Mobil, Warsteiner and Renault invite FOPA members to a slap up meal. On these occasions, members forsake the polo shirt for a smart tie bearing the famous pig logo. It is traditional at these events for Townsend to get to his feet, make a gracious speech thanking the host before making a presentation of one of these coveted ties to the host.

The club is often the subject of jokes in the paddock from other photographers, no doubt jealous at not being admitted into this brotherhood, who proudly carry the little pink pig to the four corners of the globe.

FOPA is made up of 28 photographers from 11 countries, with the addition of some mascots.

The 28 photographers:
Angelo Orsi (Italy)
Patrick Boutroux (France)
Ercole Colombo (Italy)
Frits van Eldik (Netherlands)
Martyn Elford (Great Britain)
Bruno Fablet (France)
Jimmy Froidevaux (Switzerland)
Jean-François Galeron (France)

Sandrine Haas (Belgium)
Fujio Hara (Japan)
Timo Heikkala (Finland)
Thorsten Jerg (Germany)
Hiroshi Kaneko (Japan)
Bodo Kraling (Germany)
Ferdi Kraling (Germany)
Mazakuzu Miyata (Japan)
Peter Nygaard (Denmark)
Antti Puskala (Finland)
Oliver Reck (Germany)
Daniel Reinhard (Switzerland)
José-Maria Rubio (Spain)
Rainer Schlegelmilch (Germany)
Jad Sherif (Switzerland)
Keith Sutton (Great Britain)
Mark Sutton (Great Britain)
Steven Tee (Great Britain)
John Townsend (Great Britain)
Crispin Thruston (Great Britain)

The mascots :
Ann Bradshaw (Great Britain)
Agnès Carlier (France)
Lynden Swainston (Great Britain)

One of the FOPA mascots, Agnes Carlier, with French journalist, Lionel Froissart.

The
Journalists

Bob CONSTANDUROS

If you've ever been to a Grand Prix, you will have heard the English language commentary provided by Bob Constanduros. He's been the official voice of Formula 1 since 1985. It's one of this English journalist's many jobs during a busy Grand Prix weekend.

Born in 1947, not far from Goodwood, his family was very much involved in motor sport. His father raced Singers pre-war, as did his uncle who went on to become a commentator at Le Mans and Goodwood in particular.

"I started to report club races for Autosport in 1969 as a freelance, and then joined Autosport fulltime in 1972 as club editor, going on to report Formula 3 races, touring cars and sometimes Formula 2 events.

"In 1977, I followed Jeff Hutchinson's example by buying an old VW camper, setting myself up as a photographer, and taking off as a freelance to report races all over Europe every weekend. Initially I specialised in sports cars, touring cars and Formula 2, taking in a Grand Prix when I had a free weekend.

"That was the case in 1979 at Dijon. I stayed out on the track during the closing stages of the race, because everyone else was heading back to take podium pictures, and I got loads of pics of the classic Villeneuve versus Arnoux battle." Year by year he concentrated more on Formula 1, working for Autosport, Autosport Japan, On Track in the United States and AutoHebdo in France among others. In the early eighties, he stopped taking pictures and began working with FOCA TV, conducting interviews for Bernie Ecclestone's fledgling TV company.

He was then asked to conduct the official press conferences, and in 1985, he became the on-circuit English commentator. "I've scarcely missed a race since then, nor a press conference." He also conducts new car launches each year. "The first time I had to do a presentation was at Dijon in front of 150 French people. I speak French, but my whole body was shaking like a leaf. Things have got better since then!" He also works with an American tour company with American champion Phil Hill.

Interviewing the drivers year after year means that he has an excellent rapport with them. But he still hankers after the old days and consequently takes his old camper to several races a year, including Silverstone and Nurburgring. "My colleagues really seem to appreciate it and always come to visit!" In more than 15 years of Grand Prix commentary, Bob Constanduros has never lost his voice. But equally he can't be late because races don't wait for him. "Some races are more difficult to commentate on than others. If a race is boring, you tend not to say too much although there is always the potential that something will liven it up. I've also learned not to say more than is necessary in the event of a serious accident. My uncle said too much when Stirling Moss crashed at Goodwood and lost his job. One says what one sees in such circumstances, and no more."

In spite of a busy life, Bob Constanduros has time to windsurf and ski as well us running his older son in karts. And he still has the enthusiasm and even naivety of a youngster. "I love seeing a young driver fighting the old guys but the best laugh I had was when McLaren left those silly wing covers on David Coulthard's car at Spa in 2000. I know it could have been dangerous, but I was longing for that to happen because they were born out of such paranoia! I still love the job, and hope that I can continue doing it for years to come." ∎

Gerard CROMBAC

Known in the paddock as "Jabby," this Swiss journalist is generally considered the veteran of the press room, and close friends call him simply "the legend." He has been around since the World Championship started in 1950 and is instantly recognisable with his moth eaten tweed cap, IRPA waistcoat and pipe. His laugh is often heard and is as well known as a V8 engine! "For health reasons, I've backed off a bit recently," he said, having undergone heart surgery like Bernie Ecclestone. "It's not the race weekend which is tiring, but the journeys. Now I go where I feel like, seeing about one third of the races. I like Silverstone, Monaco, Magny-Cours, Monza and Spa, the real events."

In the past, Jabby would make the trip in an old Lotus 7, sold to him by his old friend Jim Clark.

In 1949, Crombac was a mechanic for French racer Raymond Sommer, cleaning the car and doing the timing. About this time, he became a journalist. In 1950, he was the French correspondent for the English racing bible, Autosport. He also worked for other specialist magazines. In 1962, he set up Sport Auto magazine with Jean Lucas. After thirty years good and loyal service, he went into semi-retirement in 1995. Today, he produces a monthly column for Car Graphic in Japan, as well as working for publications in Indonesia, Argentina and Greece. In 1996, he celebrated his 500th Grand Prix at Magny-Cours!

Jabby always enjoyed a special relationship with the Lotus team. "I bought Jim Clark's 1963 Lotus Mk VI to race over the next few years in sports cars. I was very close to the factory and in some ways, their ambassador

in terms of negotiating start money for the 12 Hours at Reims and Le Mans, representing them in France.

Crombac and Jim Clark were great friends and even shared a flat in Paris for a while. "In 1962, I was running a supermarket and did not have much time for competing, apart from nipping up to Montlhery to qualify in my lunch hour." With a smile on his lips, Jabby continued, "In the 60s there were no press releases of course and the drivers would chase us after us so that we would write about them! The organisers did at least produce a result sheet. There was no press room, just a grandstand opposite the pits with some desks. There was a row of telephones and we queued up to dictate our copy. Then came the telex. Everyone did their own lap chart. Press rooms only evolved in the last decade or so, in fact since Bernie took control of the television in 1981."

What does Crombac think of Formula 1 in the modern era?

"It's certainly a lot less fun today. Raymond Sommer, Stirling Moss, Jim Clark, Graham Hill and Jochen Rindt were really friends. In fact, Hill and Rindt were witnesses at my wedding. After they died, I never enjoyed that sort of rapport again. I was also great friends with Francois Cevert. We were of the same generation and chased girls together." These days, I could be the drivers' grandfather," he laughs. I got on well with Jean Alesi, who reminded me of Jean Behra. Hakkinen is also a nice guy. I liked Ayrton Senna a lot and used to time his laps when he was at Lotus. I am impressed by Schumacher, but I don't find him an appealing character. To sum up, motor sport is a religion and I've got it in the blood." ■

Alan HENRY

Gerard Crombac and Alan Henry.

Jeff Hutchinson with Alan Henry in Imola in the seventies.

Born on 9th June 1947, always keen on motor sport, Alan Henry studied law with little enthusiasm. Having failed his exams, he began reporting on club meetings at Snetterton. "After two years of freelancing for Autosport, I joined Motoring News in 1970, where I covered Formula 2 races for three years." His first Grand Prix as a reporter was the British in 1973. He has been the editor of the Autocourse annual for 14 years, but on top of that, he has polished off some 38 books, the most successful being one about Ayrton Senna. "It sold quite well," said Henry modestly. His books about teams and people are works of reference. After all these years, Alan's passion is as strong as ever. "Formula 1 is in good health, as am I," he quips. "Sometimes there is too much politics, but it's still got style. During my career I have met and written about some fascinating people. I particularly like David Coulthard, Eddie Irvine, Mika Hakkinen, Alain Prost and Niki Lauda. I have absolutely no desire to do anything else and I will only go when I feel I'm being pushed." ■

Alan Henry with Niki Lauda.

Nigel ROEBUCK

I was born on 9th March 1946. My father was a doctor, but he liked motor sport. I was five when I saw my first race and I can really remember Froilan Gonzales' victory at Silverstone in 1951. Gradually, I began to get addicted. "After school, I worked in industry. Then, one day I found an American magazine called Car & Driver. I write to them offering my services. They sent me to cover the Spanish Grand Prix at Montjuich Park. They said that if they liked my work, it would be published and I'd get paid. That's how my dream became reality. A year and a half later, a new English magazine came out, called Competition Car. I was the editor, but I didn't like the job, as I had to stay in the office and did not go to races."

In 1974, he changed tack, working as press officer for Graham Hill's Ensign F1 team. At the end of the following year, the English champion was killed and the team folded. In 1976, he joined Autosport. "In 1986, I switched to working as a freelance and I am to this day, writing "Fifth Column." I also work with Autoweek in the States." After thirty years in the sport, Roebuck has no trouble picking out his favourite race. "It was the 1986 Australian Grand Prix and the title fight between Mansell, Piquet and Prost. The Frenchman won the race to take his second consecutive title. As for my favourite drivers, I would list Mario Andretti, Gilles Villeneuve, who was a great friend, Alain Prost, Keke Rosberg, Rubens Barrichello and Juan Pablo Montoya." As for the current state of the game: "there's less fun and freedom than before and the drivers watch what they say, but I not bored with it." ∎

Nigel Roebuck with Gerard Crombac.

Maurice Hamilton first saw a motor race in his native Ireland, when his father took him along to a club event. "It was a key moment for me and I was seduced by the atmosphere and the cars. In 1970, I decided to try my luck and in 1973, I went to the Monaco Grand Prix and wrote a piece from a spectator's perspective. It was published by Competition Car, whose editor was Nigel Roebuck."

In the years that followed, Hamilton did all he could to realise his dream. On 1st January 1977, he quit his sales job to join Eoin Young, working in public relations for Elf. "Right from those early days, I worked as a freelance. I became editor of Autocourse in 1978 and I was the Guardian's F1 reporter." In 1986, he switched to the Independent, but since 1990, he has worked for the Observer, as well as several other publications around the world.

"For the past 15 years, I have been the expert commentator for BBC Radio 5 Live." In his spare moments, Hamilton turns his hand to books. "I've written fifteen, including two about Jordan. My favourite is Ken Tyrrell's biography. He was the first person I interviewed back in 1977." Asked to name his favourite race, he replies the 1969 British Grand Prix and the Stewart-Rindt duel. "As a journalist, I enjoyed Japan 1994 and the following race in Australia, with the accident between Schumacher and Hill."

As for the drivers, he makes it a rule not to get too close. "In 1977 at Kyalami, I went trackside during the race and Tom Pryce was killed at my feet in horrible circumstances. All through my career, I have stuck to that principal." ■

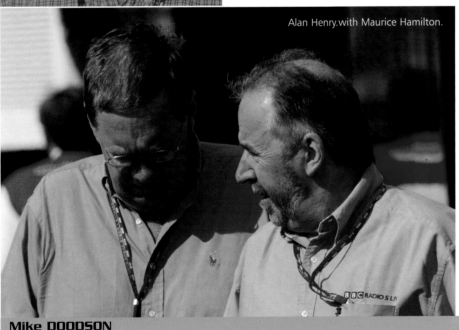

Alan Henry.with Maurice Hamilton.

62 year old Mike Doodson celebrated his 500th Grand Prix in Austria in 2003. The Toyota team even organised a little party to celebrate the event in one of its motorhomes at the track. He is one of the longest servicing journalists and, as a mathematician, photographer and accountant, he became a journalist by accident. "I'm lucky that people pay me to write. In England, it is quite common for journalists to come from all walks of life, whereas the other

nationalities in the sport seem to have trained as journalists."
Doodson began working for Motoring News at the 1969 French Grand Prix at Charade. "Then the following year, I started fulltime at the Belgian GP. That was the last year the race was held on the legendary old track. I worked for Motoring News until 1972. Then I became the first ever press officer for the JPS Lotus team. I was also freelancing for Autosport. Then I moved to Motor and onto Autocar." He now works

for a variety of publications around the world. "When I first started, I thought I would do this job for two or three years. They are still waiting for me back at the office. Then at Dijon in 1979, I thought I'd had enough. The press room did not have a single television screen, so we all went out to watch on the track. A policeman tried to move us on, saying we were in a dangerous position. That was it, I thought. But then, a few minutes later, came the fantastic duel between Villeneuve and Arnoux. So I

carried on." Doodson can still remember attending his first ever grand prix at Reims in 1959. "I was there to watch Tony Brooks win in a Ferrari." Forty years later, Doodson's heart still beats for Formula 1. That office job will have to wait. ∎

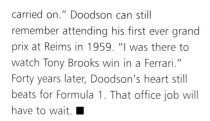

Heinz PRULLER

Heinz Pruller has all the enthusiasm of a cub reporter, but in his sixties, he has been a journalist for fifty years. "I was mad about sport and journalism and started to work for a sports paper when I was 13 and a half. I also did some radio and a bit of acting in films. When I was 15, I hitched to Maranello to interview Enzo Ferrari. It was very difficult to get hold of him, but in the end I got ten minutes of his time and he congratulated me on my tenacity."

At the age of 21, he was sports editor for a newspaper, covering skiing, football, athletics and cycling. At the time, F1 was just a hobby. He has covered around 20 winter and summer Olympic Games, several football World Cups and hundreds of ski races.

"I have attended 550 Grands Prix. Only Jabby Crombac has done more. The last time I missed a race was Hockenheim in 1994, when I was in Los Angeles for the football. He is the mainstay of Austrian television, ORF, presenting the GP programme and commentating on the race. He also writes for Kronen Zeitung, the biggest selling Austrian daily paper. The indefatigable Pruller also finds time to

fit in radio reporting and has written no less than 65 books. "I wrote the first one about Rindt in 1965 and since 1971, I have written the annual Grand Prix Story which is still going strong, with the reigning world champion usually writing the preface, or if not the job falls to Max Mosley.

He first started radio reporting at the 1965 Le Mans 24 Hours. "I was following Jochen Rindt everywhere and luckily he won, with Masten Gregory in a Ferrari. It was an excellent launch pad for my career. I knew Jochen before he was a racing driver. When he died at Monza in 1970, I decided to stop as the sport was too cruel and I had seen too many drivers die. It was the end of the world for me and I did not go to the next grand prix. But I went to the following one in Watkins Glen, where I spoke to people like Colin Chapman and Jackie Stewart and that helped me decide to carry one."

A few years later, Niki Lauda arrived on the scene, followed by Gerhard Berger. Pruller was great friends with these two and now he hopes another young Austrian star will make it to F1. "I am not chauvinistic, but I am patriotic and of course, I hope Austria will stage a grand prix again." ∎

The Photographers

Ercole Colombo, left of Rene Arnoux, at the end of the 1980 Brazilian Grand Prix.

Ercole COLOMBO

Ercole Colombo is one of the most famous photographers in Formula 1. The Italian is undoubtedly the number one in his profession and Ferrari's photographer. He was born less than two kilometres from the Monza circuit on 18th November 1944.

"I've got motor racing in the blood and when I was thirteen, me and my mates would shin over the fencing to watch the races and since those days, I've never missed an Italian Grand Prix at Monza. In 1961, I worked as a stretcher bearer, to get closer to the action. I even went to the F2 and F3 races. The Brambilla brothers lived next door and I went with them to foreign races in Monaco, Charade and Hockenheim. Jim Clark was my hero.

"I started taking pictures with my father's camera. I got married in 1969 and bought my first camera that year and the following year, after my daughter Silvia was born, I broke my leg skiing. So while I was confined to bed, I read all sorts of books about photography and with the insurance money, I bought a long lens."

He then began covering F2 and F3 races and in 1973 he attended all the European grands prix. "The following year, I also went to Brazil and from 1976, I covered the entire championship." Colombo has fond memories of those early days. "Everything was easier then. There were no pit garages and

everything took place in the open. There were no barriers and it was a smaller and more friendly world. We were very close to the drivers, they were real friends which is very rare these days."

Safety precautions were virtually nil. "In '73 at Zandvoort, Jackie Stewart complained that we were standing on the apex at the famous Tarzan corner on the actual track! We used to run across the track in the middle of the races. Our equipment meant we had to get close to the cars." While Ercole regrets the passing of that era, he admits that despite all today's restrictions, the quality of photographs is much better. "The equipment is so good that it can get round all the obstacles put in our way."

Colombo was one of the pioneers of digital photography in F1, which has lengthened a photographer's working day as it now involves transmitting all the photos to newspapers and magazines around the world from a laptop in the media centre. "I said I would give up when the computers arrived, because I am from a different age. But they came too quickly. In a couple of years, no one will use film anymore in photojournalism." ■

Rainer W. SCHLEGELMILCH

Rainer W Schlegelmich does not work for the press. He concentrates almost exclusively on producing Formula 1 books and calendars As this type of work does not fit the current FIA rules for accreditation, his Grand Prix career should have been over. But one day, Bernie Ecclestone, who has been a fan for years, said to him: "You can call me Bernie!" And he became the first photographer to carry a pass with the message, "Promotional Activities." "I thus discovered that Bernie was looking after me. In 1962, when I was 21, I had a friend who traded wine in exchange for passes and we went to the Nurburgring for the 1000 kms race. I concentrated on taking portraits rather than action shots. Before then I had no interest in racing and had no mechanical knowledge." That year he attended his first Formula 1 race at Spa. "I liked it and started sending photos to magazines." In 1964, he made a fake pass to attend the races and two years later, along with French photographer Bernard Cahier, he set up IRPA, the International Racing Press Association. As a specialist in studio work, he still considered Formula 1 as a hobby. "I would do around six grands prix per year as well as the Targa Florio and I loved Le Mans and I have attended Monaco every year since 1963. It's my favourite circuit, near the sea and one eats well."

He switched from black and white to colour at the end of the Sixties and specialised in slow exposure photos and with the arrival of zoom lenses he created his own inimitable style. Rainer's zoom shots are now famous the world over.

In around forty years of photography, he has built up a priceless library. He has produced around twenty books on Formula 1, which are real masterpieces and works of reference.

Some are even produced as numbered limited editions. He also produces calendars. "It's a good way to show off one's work."
When he started, he would shoot about ten rolls of film per race. Now he gets through eighty, maybe a hundred in Monaco. "But I am not in F1 for the money. I like to be free and independent and shoot what I like." Almost sixty, Rainer still bubbles with youthful enthusiasm. ■

Keith SUTTON

Born on 10th June 1959, Keith Sutton saw his first race at the age of six months, when he father took him to Oulton Park and at the age of four, he was snapped with Jackie Stewart who became his hero. In his youth, he was a big fan of James Hunt and all the family holidays were planned around motor racing, camping at Monaco, Le Mans and Spa. "My father was a good amateur photographer and he encouraged me to take it up. I covered my first race at Oulton

Park when I was 17 and from that day on, I knew was going to be a racing photographer. In 1980 I went freelance." A chance encounter would launch his career. "A young Brazilian had come to do the British F3 championship. He was called Ayrton Senna da Silva and we soon became friends. I did his press and promotions work and to thank me, he paid my air ticket to the 1984 Brazilian Grand Prix when he was starting his F1 career." In '85, Keith joined forces with brother Mark to form Sutton Photographic and three years later, their other brother Paul joined them too. Since 1995, the trio have operated under the banner of Sutton Motorsport Images,

employing a staff of 20, including 7 photographers. The company has several freelancers on its books to ensure global coverage of all motor sport events. After twenty years in the business, Keith retains all his enthusiasm for the sport, even though these days, his time is taken up more with dealing with clients, running the business and training new staff than with actually taking photos. "I am very lucky, travelling the world doing what I love best which is following motor racing and photography. I am under more pressure than in the early days, but as long as I'm happy I will stick at it." ■

Hiroshi KANEKO

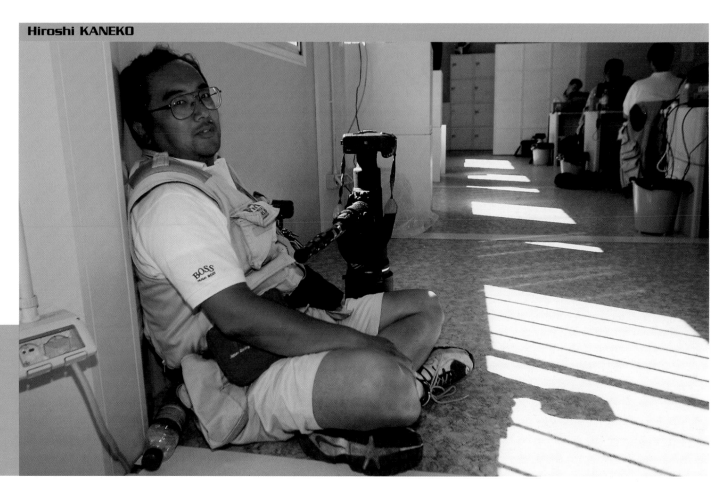

A Japanese photographer in his fifties, his Formula 1 career started with the 1976 Japanese Grand Prix at Mount Fuji. In 2002 in Canada, he celebrated his 300th grand prix. He attended his first European event at Monaco in 1978, attending just a few races. Then, in 1981, he decided to tackle it full time and left his family in Tokyo and flew to Amsterdam. He bought an old VW Combi van and travelled round Europe following the grands prix and sending his film back to Japan every Monday. It was a lonely life, given that he had very little grasp of any European language and spent many a long evening alone in his dilapidated van. At the end of the season, he would leave his van in a car park and fly home to Tokyo.

In 1982 he returned, bringing his wife with him and the two of them travelled around like gypsies and everyone recognised Kaneko-san's camper in the F1 car park. "It was great fun," he recalled. "We even cooked up Japanese meals." Strangely enough, his wife never left the bus and was never seen in the paddock, even though getting a pass was not difficult in those days.

Kaneko became famous in his native land and the arrival of Nakajima and Senna's huge popularity in Japan made Formula 1 the most popular sport in the land of the rising sun. From 1992 onwards Kaneko began travelling back to Tokyo in between every race. "It's very expensive, but I rack up plenty of air miles. I'm fed up with flying though and the jet lag on the return leg to Japan is terrible. I'm always tired." ■

Bernard ASSET

Born on 6th May 1955, Bernard Asset has always been passionate about photography and went to photo school in Paris in the 70s. "At the time, I would go on my little motorbike to motorbike races at Monthlery and the Bol d'Or to take photos. Then I came second in a competition organised by a motorbike magazine. I went to their offices to get my prize and started working for them. Then, in '73, I was asked if I was interested in cars and met the editor of Echappement magazine and started going to car races. That was the year I saw my first Formula 1 race at Silverstone."
He then continued his studies in America, returning to France to work in the darkroom

of Auto Hebdo magazine. Then in 1978, his dream came true when he landed a job with the newly launched Grand Prix International entirely devoted to Formula 1. For six years he was able to express his talent through some famous double page spreads which were the key feature of this magazine. He brought a fresh and artistic angle and found a new way of illustrating the sport. A specialist in low speed action and photos capturing movement and atmosphere, his work has inspired many. A true artist, Asset refuses to go digital. "I am a devotee of film. I come from the old school, but one day I will have to go digital, although I keep putting it off." In 2003 at Monaco, he finally took the plunge. ■

Jean-François Galeron, Jad Sherif and Maza Deshima in 1983.

Jad SHERIF

Born on 25th March 1957 in Beirut, Jad Sherif spent his early years travelling the globe with his parents, before studying photography in London. "I was mad about Formula 1 and photography. I would go down to Brands Hatch to watch F1 testing and one day I rang Autosport looking for work. They suggested I contact a journalist called Jeff Hutchinson who was looking for a photographer. He was based in France, near the Swiss border, which was ideal as my parents were based in Geneva. The first GP I worked at was the 1981 Dutch GP and the following year I did the whole season."
By 1985, not only was Sherif doing all the F1 grands prix, he was also covering 90% of the motorcycle grands prix. The word "holiday" did not figure in his vocabulary, but at least he got to travel in Hutchinson's own private plane!

"In 1990, I set up my own agency, Pan Images and Jeff Hutchinson effectively became my client. Working for myself was more motivating." Today, Jad runs his own lab near Geneva. "I have an exciting life and I accept the constraints, which are not having a private life and working at the weekends. But it beats working in an office and racing is my passion. I don't know how long I will continue. The economic climate and my physical condition will be the deciding factors." In 2003, Sherif joined forces with fellow photographers Jean-Francois Galeron and Laurent Charniaux. "We set up World Racing Images, which concentrates on the grands prix and all the major international motor races. Our site, www.worldracingimages.com means that our clients can go on line to chose photos at their convenience." ■

Steven TEE

The Tee family has been involved in motor sport for decades. Steven's grandfather was the founder of the English magazines, Motorsport and Motoring News. In 1948, Steven's father became a photographer, setting up LAT, London Art Technical. Steven started work in motor racing at the age of twenty. He covered national races in England and attended his first grand prix at Imola in 1984. "I haven't missed any since.." Steven is now the boss of LAT which has a library of around six million photos. "It's the biggest archive in the world, with photos dating back to 1901." Tee plus four other photographers and a technician now attend every grand prix. "Apart from media work we work with five F1 teams: McLaren, Williams, Renault and Toyota and we are doing more and more digital photography, although being of the old school, I still prefer film. I still love my work, but I am planning to take a bit of a back seat before I turn fifty. It's a physically demanding job." ■

Giorgio
PIOLA

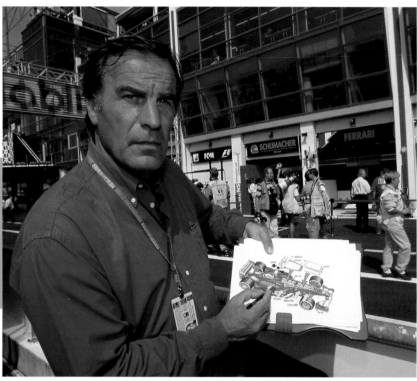

An elegant and classy Italian from near Genoa, the perma-tanned Giorgio Piola is one of the more stylish members of the F1 media. Technical drawing is his domain and although often copied, he has never been equalled by some of his compatriots who have tried to provide a similar service. He is the undoubted master of his craft. For over twenty years, he has been drawing Formula 1 cars and he has nothing to prove. These days, the cars can change from one race to the next, but nothing escapes his attention. Armed with a keen eye for detail, a little camera, pencils and a computer he commits these changes to paper race after race. He has no special access to the cars, which makes his work all the more remarkable. As a motor racing fan, he saw his first grand prix at Monaco in 1969, when his other passion was already drawing. "All my family could draw well and I was drawing cars since I was 16 years old." In 1974, armed with an engineering degree, he had a bet with a friend and won a competition organised by Automundo magazine. He was invited to attend the Italian Grand Prix to produce a photo and drawing report. In 1976, he did a season of Formula

Ford racing in a Tecno with a rear end he designed himself, but when it came to driving, he was not very talented. "But it gave me the experience to learn more about racing cars."

In 1978, he worked with Arturo Merzario when the Italian was building his own cars. "I was not really an engineer, but I could make myself understood by everyone."

The little Italian driver with his cowboy hat screwed permanently on his head did not spend long in Formula 1 and so Piola turned to journalism. For over 20 years, he has worked with several quality newspapers and magazines around the world (Auto Sprint, Gazzeta dello Sport, Sport Auto, F1 Magazine and others.)

"From each race, I have to supply between four to six drawings and an explanatory story by Sunday morning. I try to use simple language so that all the readers can understand. In the 1970s, it took about twenty days to do one drawing. Now it takes just a few hours."

Nevertheless, Piola sometimes has some sleepless nights and a hotel room is not always the best drawing studio. As well as this magazine work, every year he also

produces a technical guide: "Technical Analysis of the F1 season," which is published in Italian and English. It is a veritable Bible for technical fans. It covers the sport team by team with all the details of engines, suspension and aerodynamics. The shape of engine covers and wings are all scrupulously detailed race by race. "This book has won a prize for best book of the year in Italy and I have also been recognised as the best Italian journalist."

These days, Formula 1 is a paranoid environment. McLaren has installed a system of surveillance cameras to check for spies. "I get on well with the engineers, even though my job is to unveil their secrets. Sometimes, for example, Williams technical director Patrick Head teases me by saying there is something new on the car to see if I can spot it! I have to admit that McLaren and Ferrari sometimes get annoyed when I discover and publish their latest modification."

Despite ever more sophisticated surveillance systems and the covers which hide the cars, Piola carries on working, using his little digital camera. No secrets ever escape him. "I am the technology paparazzi!" ■

The Radio Reporter

Jonathan LEGARD (BBC)

One event that stands out from Legard's seven years at the races is the 1998 Belgian Grand Prix at Spa. "It was raining at the start and there was that huge accident after the start on the run down past the old pits Then there was the crash between Coulthard and Schumacher and finally a win for Damon Hill. I loved that race." Away from the races, he does not get to spend that much time with his family. "I am responsible for everything to do with F1 in terms of news. I have to prepare my programme and look after my section on the BBC web site, so I'm quite busy." After Indianapolis in 2002, when Ferrari stage managed the finish, he felt a bit bored with it all. Schumacher's crushing dominance had taken something out of the sport. "Luckily, everything has been much better in 2003, with six different winners in the first nine races. Now, each session counts and everyone has to plan their race. But at first, I did not like the new timetable, but I can see I was wrong. The racing is much more interesting, but for the commentators, qualifying is now a difficult job. You need a lot of information and have to think about the different strategies the drivers might adopt. It is a new challenge for us too." ■

I n his forties, living in London, Jonathan Legard commentates on the Formula 1 Grands Prix for BBC radio.
"I started at the BBC in 1996. I was living in Liverpool and commentated on the local Everton football matches. That year, I moved to London, presenting programmes on the Olympic Games, the Ryder Cup in golf, the Commonwealth Games and the Euro 96 football series."
Always a big fan of Formula 1 and Niki Lauda in particular, naturally he dreamed of working at the grands prix. "I was lucky enough to start commentating on F1 starting in 1997 and I have done it ever since. The BBC does live broadcasts of Friday and Saturday qualifying and of course, the race. On top of that, I present a weekly programme lasting half an hour called 5 Live F1, which goes out on Friday nights. We have all sorts of guests, like Bernie, Frank Williams and Ron Dennis. "At the track, we go on air five minutes before each session. Luckily, unlike some of my foreign colleagues, I am not alone. I work with our expert Maurice Hamilton, Peter Slater in the pits and the producer, Jason Swales."

The **Media** Centres

Imola 2002.

Silverstone 2000.

Magny-Cours 2000.

This is the place the journalists call home. The FIA provides the grands prix organisers with a list of requirements which gets ever more demanding, as to what is required to help the ever increasing number of journalists do their job.

Every afternoon, from Thursday to Sunday, a press conference is held, bringing together various drivers and team personnel, although on Saturday and Sunday the standard format is to have the top three drivers from qualifying and the top three finishers in the race respectively.

The BAR press officer hands out the team press release to the journalists.

Salle de presse en Autriche.

Magny-Cours 1999.

Indianapolis 2000.

Barcelone 2000.

In each media centre, journalists can find the team press releases, as well as all the time sheets and facts and figures from each session and the race.

Malaysia 2002.

Nürburgring 2003.

Nürburgring 2000.

The **Press** Officers

The role involves maintaining the relationship between the team and the media. The job seems to be growing, with the big teams employing several people in this role. Drivers and the big sponsors also have their own press people. These days, it is impossible to organise an interview without passing through the intermediary of a press officer.

Sabine KEHM

She is very much in demand as the person in charge of all Michael Schumacher's dealings with the media from all over the world. Having studied sports journalism, she worked for Die Welt, one of Germany's three biggest daily papers. She was multi-tasked, covering tennis, skiing, football and the Olympics. In 1994, she discovered Formula 1 at Hockenheim and by 1997 this was the only sport she covered. "I really wanted to work for the Suddentsche Zeitung paper, which is the biggest in Germany. Then, one day in 1999, I got a phone call from Michael Schumacher's manager, Willi Weber, who offered me the job of being his driver's press manager." After giving it some thought, she took on this fascinating task which is certainly demanding, starting in her new position at the start of 2000.

"Officially, I'm a media consultant. I look after all Michael's dealings with press and public relations. I also give my advice when it comes to selecting personal sponsors. In simple terms, I look after all Michael's work with the public."

Kehm is 38 years old and lives in Berlin and spends very little time there, as she follows her driver everywhere. "I go to all the races, all the test sessions and all his public appearances. Luckily, for the past few years, he spends November and December with his family and so I can get a breather."

Sabine works closely with Ferrari's head of motor sport PR, Luca Colajanni and his department.

She will not be drawn on the precise number of requests she receives for interviews. "In Germany, all the newspapers are looking for a meeting and it is not realistic to satisfy everyone. During the race weekends, Michael does not have much time for the media, apart from meetings organised by Ferrari and the TV interviews after the press conferences. Lack of time means that exclusive interviews have become a rarity and are done mainly at private test sessions where he usually has more time. We have to group the journalists together according to their nationality to meet the demand."

This year, Kehm has written a book, the first on which Schumacher really collaborated. "We had several projects on the go and it seemed logical that we could do a book. He looked at me and said 'why not?' Called "Driving Force" it reveals another side to the champion, with photos from the famous French photographer Michel Comte, showing Michael enjoying time with his wife and children. There is not much F1 in the book, but fans will see Michael's private life." Spending so much time with the five times world champion means Sabine Kehm has been through some exciting times. "I particularly remember when he won his first title with Ferrari in 2000 at Suzuka. It was my first year working with him. It was a joyous and very special moment and I had never experienced such emotion. Seeing him cry in the press conference at Monza was also memorable. There were many more."

Sabine Kehm does not hide the fact this is a tiring job and her contract expires at the end of 2004. "Maybe I will also be negotiating an extension to my contract," she says with a laugh. "But it is so tiring that sometimes I think I might like to become a journalist again." ■

Ellen KOLBY

From the west coast of Denmark, Ellen Kolby has lived in England since 1990. Having lived with here parents in the United States, at the age of 18 she read politics and history at Manchester University before doing a Masters in journalism in London.

"In 1995, my sister Kirsten was competing in the British Formula Renault series and my brother Christian was karting. So I got involved in motor racing. On race weekends, I helped them out doing press releases and I met the people running the Vauxhall series. When I finished my Masters, I was offered a job with CSS Promotions, where I became press officer for the Vauxhall Opel series and Formula Junior. At this time, I first came into contact with drivers like Ralph Firman, Justin Wilson and Mark Webber." Then came a stint in the British Touring Car series, followed by a job with Prism where she did PR for Ford's involvement in Formula 1, looking after the Stewart team. "Then, in 1999 I was contacted by the McLaren team and had several interviews before reaching an agreement at Monza, after six months of discussion. I finished the year with Stewart Grand Prix in Japan and started work for McLaren the following week."

For the past four years, she has been in charge of communications for McLaren and the TAG McLaren Group, which involves looking after seven companies along with a staff of four. "I do all the public relations, press relations and also work with the sponsors in terms of the media. I also look after the team's Internet site. To sum it up, I centralise all McLaren's media interests. When she started work with McLaren, Kolby moved to Woking, close to the factory. "I didn't really like living there, so I moved back to London and commute."

Between races, she attends several test sessions and various promotional events, so life is never dull. For the grands prix, Kolby usually travels out on a Tuesday for events outside Europe and Wednesday for the others, depending on any promotional commitments.

"Travelling can be tiring, but I like moving around. For a while, my sister worked at BAR and my brother raced in F3000, so I would see them at the races. I'm 32 so I don't know when I will stop this fascinating but demanding work. The McLaren group is active in many areas and there is plenty to keep me occupied, including the nearly completed Paragon Centre and the road going McLaren-Mercedes SLR." ■

Silvia FRANGIPANE-HOFFER

orn on 7th August 1965, Italian Silvia Frangipane has always liked motor racing. "I got a degree in architecture in Milan in 1989. Then I worked for Bugatti in PR. I stayed until 1996 before joining Ducati in 1997 where I was in charge of Public Relations. One day, a journalist who knew Giancarlo Minardi well told me he was looking for a press officer for Formula 1. I met Mr. Rumi, who had bought the team and I started work in F1 in 1998. During the season, I learnt that Williams was looking for someone who spoke Italian and German, as they had taken on Zanardi and BMW had arrived. Frank Williams spoke to Minardi. As Gabriele Rumi's niece Stefania Torelli had just been taken on, I was available."

So, Silvia found herself working for one of the top Formula 1 teams after just a year in the business. "Giancarlo Minardi taught me everything. He explained everything, such as how to read the timing monitor. He never got angry, even though I made a lot of mistakes at first. He was always very kind and I owe him a lot."

She started working for Williams at Imola in 1999. Her beaming smile is a key element of the team. Last year at Imola again, she attended her last race before taking maternity leave and is now mother to Veronique. She returned to work for the 2002 Australian Grand Prix. "I lived in England until I had my daughter and since then I moved back to Italy, as my husband is a ski instructor at Madonna di Campiglio. We live in the mountains and next to Lake Garda.

"I don't need to go to the factory, except when they ask me to. I can work from home and travel to all the grands prix and some test sessions and I plan my job around my daughter. I work in the evenings and on Sundays. There is a lot of work at Williams, whereas at Minardi, hardly any journalists turned up for the press briefings. But it was a challenge and you had to work hard to get results."

There is no time to get bored at Williams. Silvia looks after all relations with the journalists as regards the team and drivers. She writes all the press releases after talking to the drivers and the Williams and BMW management. Then she distributes copies in the media centre; around 200 in English and 50 in German.

An American company sends the releases by e-mail to around a thousand addresses. She also organises driver press conferences, with television being the priority. Juan Pablo Montoya is much in demand and there is a very long waiting list as he rarely does one-to-ones, except for TV. So most of the interviews are done in groups. A Brazilian journalist has been waiting a year to talk to him. However, Ralf Schumacher does one to ones at test sessions. "I have to organise the waiting list which isn't always simple." Apart from Italian, Silvia speaks French, English and German. " I can manage Spanish when I've had a couple of drinks."

For races outside Europe, she arrives a week before the race, but only on Thursday for those in Europe. Mondays after a grand prix are very busy. "I have four weeks holiday a year, but I have difficulty fitting them in. There is always something to do. Our press and marketing department is very small, just ten of us. McLaren has five times that number."

In some ways, the race weekend is less stressful. "I have a bit more time and am always available. Silverstone is the toughest grand prix and TV crews come to the factory which is not that far from the track." ■

Silvia with Giancarlo Minardi.

BAn Australian from Melbourne, Jules Kulpinski was press attache for Danni Minogue and when invited to the 1999 Spanish Grand Prix by British American Tobacco, they met Jacques Villeneuve. "After that, I started working for Jacques as well as Danni. I look after all Jacques' press work. At the end of 1999 I was faced with a big decision and I chose motor racing. I have been interested in Formula 1 since I was sixteen, but I never thought I would make a career out of it. It happened by accident."
Kulpinski accompanies her driver to all his professional engagements. As Jacques, like David Coulthard prefers to stay in his own motorhome when at the circuits, she drives by and picks him up every morning to take him to the paddock and she does not leave until

he does. All media requests have to pass through her. "I go to all the races and tests and the promo events, which he doesn't really like doing. I work closely with the BAR press department." She also sees to Villeneuve's web site www.jv-world.com and runs his diary. In Canada, Villeneuve is a legend. "It's the hardest race for me with press conferences to organise in town and a great deal of media interest to cope with from the locals. Of course, my favourite race is Melbourne. I can stay at home and it's also the first race of the season, so it's a bit like going back to school. It's a very well run event. Kulpinski now lives in Oxford, but she is away more than 200 days per year. "I am never tired or bored as I love travelling." ■

Severine Ray was born on 18th June 1970. After attending business school, she worked for the Bayer laboratories, in charge of medical visits. She then went to Morocco. "I soon got bored with that, so I took a sabbatical going to England where I did translations. Then I moved to Canada. Back in France, I got a job with Michelin in September 1977. I was looking after internal communications for one of the factories. I had no idea of working in sport." But that's what happened two years later. In June 1999 she joined the press department working under Andy Pope.
"Four days after I arrived, I was off to Greece for the Acropolis Rally before heading for Le Mans. Then, I started attending the grands prix in F1. Before our return in 2000, we had to learn all about this new challenge in terms of marketing and hospitality. Formula 1 was nothing new to me. My father had a factory in Coventry, England, making parts for a lot of constructors involved in F1. He was a friend of Patrick Depailler's. I was six years old and he

often took me to the grands prix. I also knew Jacques Lafitte and Eddie Jordan through my father. When I returned, some aspects were familiar but there were a lot of changes. There were no more chip shops in the paddock." From the start of 2000, Severine was facing a big challenge. "I was all alone to look after the press, the hospitality and public relations, whereas in the other teams, there are several people to tackle these various tasks. I was going mad trying to think of something interesting to write in the press releases, without giving away any secrets. It was a case of saying something but not too much. At first I was writing reams. Now, I only do short statements from Pierre Dupasquier or Pascal Vasselon. It's simple and easy to use for the journalists."
Ray was pleasantly surprised by the welcome she got. "I had been told that F1 had become a closed world. But I was not regarded as an

intruder and there was no hostility or austerity in the paddock." Ray has little free time. "As well as doing all the press releases I also look after the Michelin Internet site, keeping it updated. I don't have any drivers to look after, just Pierre Dupasquier and Pascal Vasselon. I do all the work connected with running a press office." ■

With Anne Giuntini, a journalist with the French daily paper, "L'Equipe."

The Television itv

James ALLEN

James Allen was born in November 1966. Aged 25, he became press officer for the Brabham team. At the end of 1991, he switched to journalism, working for Autosport. Two years later, he became an F1 reporter for the American ESPN television channel, before joining ITV as pit lane reporter in 1997. In 2001, he took on the daunting task of replacing the living legend that is Murray Walker as the main commentator. "Commentating on a grand prix is a tough job. You cannot give the viewers a load of indigestible facts and figures on a Sunday afternoon. There is also no need to tell them what they can see for themselves. Our job is more a case of explaining and analysing strategies, dabbling in news and giving opinions. I enjoy a perfect understanding with Martin Brundle, whom I worked with when he was a Brabham driver.

The new qualifying rules make our job more complicated, trying to tell the viewers about the different fuel levels being used and analysing tyre choice. Doing it live means having to be very clear and precise.

"It might seem as though I'm paid to just talk a bit, but there is a lot of background work, attending all the press conferences and chasing stories, even the anodyne ones. All I know is that I won't go on until I'm 78, like my predecessor, Murray did." ∎

In a truck belonging to the SFP (Societe Francaise de Production) the images from the French Grand Prix are broadcast from various camera positions around the track.

Louise GOODMAN

Born in Alresford, Hampshire, Louise Goodman learnt to drive on her father's knee at the age of four, enthusiastically twiddling the wheel of the family Morris Traveller.

Her journalistic career began on a powerboat magazine. In 1987, she switched to Formula 1, working for Tony Jardine's PR agency, looking after Camel's tie-up with the Lotus team and Ayrton Senna. "I started going to races in 1988, working with Piquet and Nakajima. The following year, I became Camel's press officer. Still working for Jardine Communications, I switched to the Leyton House team and in 1992, I followed Ian Phillips to Jordan, working as press officer until 1997. When ITV took over the TV rights from the BBC, I was asked to join their team of reporters and was assigned to cover the action in the pits."

Apart from commentary, Louise also works on features and interviews, producing the clips in the TV Compound at the races. "It's an exciting job as live TV puts you under a lot of pressure and is a big adrenaline rush. Of course, I have a good relationship with the British drivers. I worked with Rubens Barrichello for a long time at Jordan and I still like interviewing him. I also get on well with Montoya, but generally I get on fine with all the drivers. Even Kimi Raikkonen, who is not the chattiest, can be persuaded to do a good interview."

As her partner is Minardi's Sporting Director, John Walton, Goodman's life revolves around Formula 1. Rallying is also a passion and she has co-driven for Tony Jardine and driven in the British Ford Ka series. "I know I'm lucky to have

Tony Jardine with Fernando Alonso and Jenson Button.

worked in this world for over a decade. Life in the paddock is full of mystery and I wrote a book about it a few years back, looking at life behind the scenes during the 2000 season." At forty years of age, Louise still loves her work. "I never get bored. I am always learning something and still as enthusiastic as ever." ■

Tony JARDINE

Communications is Tony Jardine's forte and, in his fifties, there is little he does not know about Formula 1, which he puts to good use in his role as ITV's consultant.

"When I was 7, I was a Stirling Moss fan, then Jim Clark became my favourite. I even saw him race. Once, at an F3 race, I managed to get Jackie Stewart's autograph three times!"

An art and architecture teacher, Jardine worked in Liverpool, Kuwait, Teheran and Michigan. But he was always keen on racing, campaigning a Formula Ford while studying. In 1975, he quit teaching, returning to England. "I was a truck driver for six months and then I got a job with Goodyear. In '76, I was truckie and a tyre fitter. The following year I was an engineer and then became team coordinator for Brabham, working on

the BT49 with Gordon Murray." In 1980, Jardine moved to McLaren as assistant team manager. "But when Ron Dennis bought the team, I was shown the door in no uncertain terms: 'You, out!'"

He then contacted John Player Special to take on a marketing role with Lotus. "I was looking after Mansell and De Angelis, as well as Barry Sheene on two wheels and powerboats. Then, I became press officer at Lotus, also looking after sponsors. That year, I set up Jardine Communications. "I landed the contract for the Virgin transatlantic record attempt."

When Peter Warr took over Lotus after the death of Colin Chapman, the team signed with Camel and Jardine was called in as an adviser, beating off more established agencies. "It was a great time, working with Senna again. We also looked after the F3000 team and the famous Camel Trophy."

Jardine picked up several other F1 accounts and now runs a staff of 25, who also work in other sports. "But I have still continued doing TV and radio work. I was in the pits for the BBC and did six years with FOCA TV. Now I am a studio analyst for ITV." Full of energy, Jardine still finds time to compete on rallies and races and nothing phases him, a smile permanently on his lips as he cruises the paddock, enjoying his passion for the sport. ■

Circuit de Catalunya

Access to the TV Compound is very strictly controlled.

A view of the TV. compound.

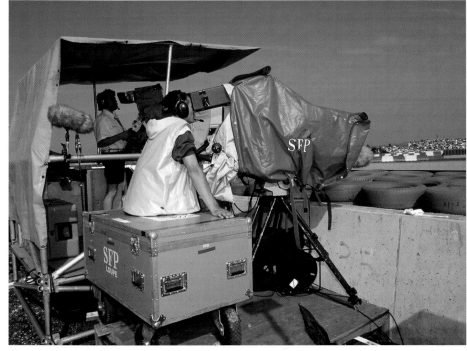

4
THE
PEOPLE

THE PEOPLE

They are an essential part of the paddock. While this book is not exhaustive, Formula 1 owes a great deal to these people who work in a variety of different jobs.

The Federation Internationale de l' Automobile

A group photo of all the FIA personnel who work at the track.

The FIA was set up in 1904 and today it boasts a membership of 157 clubs and federations, representing 118 countries. Its authority covers two distinct areas. The first concerns the every day use of cars on the road; safety, the environment and traffic. The second, of more interest in this context is its sporting powers. The FIA is more or less the international governing body for all forms of motor sport and of course, Formula 1 is its flagship. In the paddock, it deploys a certain number of key people.

Max MOSLEY

The President of the FIA, he is elected by the presidents of each club or federation. He is a lawyer who knows his motor racing, as he raced in Formula 2 in the 60s. He was one of the founders of the March Formula 1 team, his initial being the first letter of a name, which became an institution in the world of racing. In Formula 1, he came to know Bernie Ecclestone, who had just bought the Brabham team. Together, they created the constructors' organisation, FOCA. The war between the constructors and Jean-Marie Balestre, president of the FISA (Federation Internationale du Sport Automobile) would be a long one.

Having buried the hatchet, Mosley became president of FISA in 1991, and two years later he headed the FIA. He is the architect of the Concorde Agreement which binds all the teams together in their dealings with the sporting authority. He is a great diplomat who makes the best use of his legal talents to steer round obstacles.

Bernie ECCLESTONE

We have dealt with him already. He is vice-president of the FIA and holds the purse strings. He is the big money man of F1. (see pages 124-127).

Martin Brundle and Max Mosley after a run in the McLaren two-seater at Silverstone circuit in 1998.

Max Mosley and Bernie Ecclestone.

Charlie Whiting in conversation with Juan Pablo Montoya.

Jo Bauer

inspection prior to every practice session and the race. He is also the head of the Formula 1 technical department. All modifications made to a circuit must have his approval. Finally, he is personally in control of the start procedure, controlling the red lights which unleash the pack of monsters.

Charlie WHITING

An Englishman who has been Race Director since 1997. He was chief mechanic with the Brabham team for ten years from 1977 to '87. He was then appointed technical delegate with the FIA and is in charge of circuit safety. At the wheel of a super powerful Mercedes CLK, he carries out a track

The German was unknown until the famous Ferrari barge board incident at the 1999 Malaysian Grand Prix.
He is the FIA technical delegate at all the races and along with Michel Lepraist oversees, along with other FIA staff, all the draconian scrutineering checks carried out by local officials at each track.

Charlie Whiting also acts as the official starter for the race.

In the scrutineering garage, Jo Bauer and Michel Lepraist take a close look at the Williams-BMW.

Charlie Whiting (on left) in 1984.

Herbie BLASH

Bernie Ecclestone likes to work with people he knows well. Like Charlie Whiting and Eddie Baker, 52 year old Blash is also a former Brabham man. He is the assistant race director and there is nothing he does not know about Formula 1.
He looked after Jochen Rindt's car at Lotus, before becoming Brabham team manager in the days of Nelson Piquet. From there, he moved to fronting Yamaha's F1 operation before joining the FIA.

Sid WATKINS

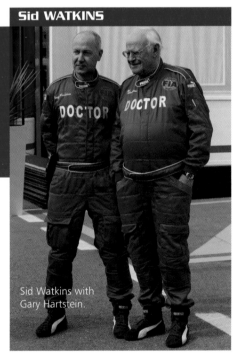

Sid Watkins with Gary Hartstein.

Mentioned at length elsewhere in this book, the English neurosurgeon has officiated in Formula 1 for over twenty years. He is the official Grand Prix doctor, assisted by the American Gary Harstein and Frenchman Jacques Issermann. Jean-Marie Balestre was the first to pay particular attention to driver medical care. Then, after the deaths of Ayrton Senna and Roland Ratzenberger and Karl Wendlinger's accident, the safety commission, presided over by Sid Watkins intensified its research.

Cockpit protection, driver extraction still in the seat, the drivers' legs moved to a point behind the front wheel axle are just some of the measures introduced by "Prof" and his team and safety has much improved in recent years thanks to their efforts.

Bernd MAYLÄNDER

The 31 year old German used to be a specialist in the Porsche SuperCup which runs as a curtain-raiser to the grands prix. Today, he drives the Mercedes Safety Car, which goes round the track prior to the start of the race and is also called out in case of a problem, when Maylander has to keep all the cars running behind him until the track is fit to race again.

Jacques TROPENAT

The Frenchman is an excellent "gentleman racer" and a doctor, who acts as Sid Watkins' chauffeur in the Mercedes Medical Car at the grands prix.

Richard WOODS

The Englishman replaced Francesco Longanesi after the 2002 Spanish Grand Prix as FIA's director of communications and the man in charge of public relations.

Agnes KAISER

Agnes Kaiser prepares the passes.

A Frenchwoman responsible for FIA's relationship with the journalists and written media. After working for Peugeot Sport, she took over PR work for the France GT championship with Patrick Peter in 1997 and 1998. In November that year, she joined the FIA external affairs department, looking after international accreditation. At the start of 1999, this department moved from Paris to Geneva. At the end of '99, Kaiser was appointed F1 press delegate. At the grands prix, she ensures that the FIA carnet de charge is carried out as far as the media centre is concerned, as well as supervising media accreditation. She has the final say when it comes to national press accreditation. She provides FOM with a list of names so that the credentials can be manufactured and sent out 10 days before each grand prix. There is no quota for written media, other than the constraints of having the room to accommodate them.

However, only 30 international and 12 national photographers are accredited per race, as the FIA tries to ensure the highest standards and only wants true professionals. On site, Kaiser checks that all is in order in the media centre and that all press credentials are available in the accreditation centre. From Thursday onwards, she ensures that press conferences and TV unilateral interviews run smoothly, as well as dealing with parking problems. Kaiser also controls the distribution of the FIA News bulletins and all time and results sheets. Finally, she also updates the FIA Internet site. "My role is to promote our championship, to ensure its strong image and to attend to the needs of the journalists." The highest number of accreditation requests are for Monaco, Imola, Barcelona,

Hockenheim and Budapest. On the other side of the coin, Sao Paulo, Sepang, Montreal and Suzuka are less popular. "In fact, it all depends on the state of the championship and whether or not the titles have already been decided. The record for the highest number of accreditations came in 1999."

Pat BEHAR

This French former F1 photographer has been in charge of relations between the FIA and photographers for around ten years. He works in close collaboration during the year with the race organisers to ensure that a very precise cahier de charge regarding photographers viewing points around the circuit is adhered to. Born on 15th October 1948 in Marseille, he decided to go and live in the United States. He began his photographic career at the 1977

Long Beach Grand Prix. "Taking photos was a childhood dream. I started when I was 27 and I am self-taught. At that time, there was no problem getting a pass. I just covered the grands prix in the States." In 1984, he returned to Europe and for 10 years he covered nearly all the grands prix for various agencies such as Vandystadt, Press Sports, DPPI and Tempsport. In 1994, he hung up his cameras when he was appointed photographers representative with the FIA. He is in charge of attributing the passes within the required quota. "Sometimes there are twice as many requests as there are places. It can be a nightmare sorting them out." He arrives at the circuit on the Monday before the race for the races outside Europe and on Tuesday for the others. He supervises the set up of the photographers area, the start tower and the general working conditions for the photographers at the track. "These jobs all have their good and their bad points. I would still like to be a photographer. But the hardest part was the selling…" Between them, these two people sort out all the inevitable problems to do with passes and have to deal with the eternally unsatisfied media.

The FIA team at all the grands prix is completed by two technical assistants, Claudio Garavini and Michel Lepraist, data analysts Simon Busby and Alan Prudom and a fuel analyst, Peter Tibbets. Sally Paxton is Charlie Whiting's assistant and secretary to the Stewards, while Gwenda Searle ensures everything runs smoothly over the weekend. ■

Bernie ECCLESTONE

The Avenue leading to the Hungaroring.

1974: Bernie Ecclestone is the owner of the Brabham team. Here he talks with his driver, Carlos Reutemann.

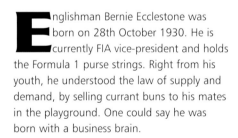

Englishman Bernie Ecclestone was born on 28th October 1930. He is currently FIA vice-president and holds the Formula 1 purse strings. Right from his youth, he understood the law of supply and demand, by selling currant buns to his mates in the playground. One could say he was born with a business brain.

After the war, he set up a motorcycle dealership and business was good. Bernie already had his own unique selling methods. In the shop window, all the bikes were neatly lined up with the front wheels pointing the same way at exactly the same angle. He then moved on to running a second hand car dealership, while trying his hand at motorbike racing, without too much success. In 1949, he switched to four wheels. He bought a Formula 3, then a Cooper which used to belong to Mike Hawthorn. Ecclestone soon realised he would not find fame and fortune

as a driver, but he competed as a gentleman driver for several years, with the highspots being failed attempts to qualify at the Monaco and British Grands Prix in 1958 in a Connaught. He owned the team, which he bought when it went bankrupt the previous winter.

He then managed the career of the young Stuart Lewis-Evans who drove a Vanwall. The death of his protégé at Casablanca in the 1958 Moroccan Grand Prix had a profound effect on Ecclestone. He stayed away from racing for around a decade. During this time his business affairs prospered and he moved into estate agency as his fortune grew. Rumours still circulate in England that he was the brains behind the Great Train Robbery back in 1963, although no evidence has ever come to light.

In 1968, he met the Austrian driver, Jochen Rindt and acted as his manager, with a view to creating their own team. Rindt's fatal

accident at Monza in 1970 signalled another halt in Ecclestone's racing ambitions. Two years later, he was back, buying the Brabham team. It was not an easy start and the cars only began to show signs of promise in 1974.

One year later, Ecclestone set up the Formula One Constructors Association, the famous FOCA organisation. It was created to protect the interests of the teams when dealing with race organisers. "At the time, the circuit owners only gave us start money which did not even cover the transport costs." FOCA's president would soon become the real power in Formula 1. He managed to sell the grid in its entirety to the organisers, taking a percentage of whatever deal he struck. FOCA regularly increased its rates for start and prize money.

Bernie and his British affiliate teams were doing very well indeed. However, relations with the governing body got complicated

Colin Chapman, the genial boss of the Lotus team, with Bernie Ecclestone in 1979.

With Charlie Whiting, his chief mechanic in 1986.

With Jean-Marie Balestre.

when Jean-Marie Balestre became head of FISA, the Federation Internationale du Sport Automobile. The presence of major manufacturers like Renault, Alfa Romeo and Fiat behind the Ferrari badge was a worry to the smaller teams, all reliant on the Ford V8 engine, up against the turbocharged units of the newcomers. The FOCA teams were not prepared to go down this route and got as far as proposing their own championship. Enzo Ferrari himself had to intervene to save the World Championship. The start of the 80s was marked by cataclysmic and vitriolic discussions between Ecclestone and Balestre. It seemed that the sport was not big enough for the both of them. After his election, Jean-Marie Balestre had but one idea in mind. He wanted to reassert the power of FISA in the face of FOCA and

Max Mosley with Flavio Briatore.

Spa 1999: Deep in conversation with Eddie Jordan and Tom Walkinshaw, Bernie holds plans for the new BAR. He had forgotten he was in the middle of the pack and the confidential document would soon be seen by all.

The "Bernies" are awarded for outstanding contributions to Formula 1.

With Shaquile O'Neal.

The hatchet has been buried for quite a while with Jean-Marie Balestre.

Ecclestone. It was open war and Formula 1 did not come out of it very well. It led to the signing of the Concorde Agreement which gave FOCA control of F1 finances, leaving the sporting regulations to FISA. In 1991, Max Mosley, a long time friend of Bernie Ecclestone took over as president of FIA and, so far, has ensured lasting peace in Formula 1.

But Bernie has never been one to keep all his eggs in one basket. Shortly after the creation of FOCA, he was the first to tackle the issue of television rights. It was an excellent way of promoting F1 and as the figures involved grew ever bigger, it became an excellent source of revenue for the teams.

Ecclestone also set up Allsport Management, with Patrick McNally at the helm. This company looks after trackside advertising and runs the Paddock Club; both enterprises

proving very profitable. Ecclestone always looks to go further and in 1996, he set up his own pay-per-view satellite television company. It offered more extensive coverage than terrestrial television. Bernie invested huge sums of money into this enterprise, but so far it has not paid off.

Does he ever think about retirement? "Elvis is dead, but the show goes on and the same will happen with F1 when I retire." The question as to who will succeed Bernie has been discussed for a long time now and the conclusion is that he cannot be replaced by just one man, with some sort of board of directors required to look after the business. In 1998, he underwent a triple heart bypass operation and a few weeks later, he was back at work, holding meetings in his metallic grey motorhome in the heart of the paddock. His wife Slavica and his two daughters often come along too.

There are some who criticise his methods. His detractors say he is heartless, which is certainly not the case. He has never forgotten his former employees and several members of the Brabham team are still by his side today or working for the FIA. For example, Charlie Whiting is now race director at the grands prix and Eddie Baker and Herbie Blash also occupy key roles in the sport. Criticism is easy to understand, given the personal fortune he

has built up over the years. One could accuse him of pushing up the costs of anything connected with the sport. Thanks to him, a lot of the British "garagistes" have also become incredibly wealthy. For example, at the end of the 70s, Frank Williams was on the edge of the abyss looking in and had to sell everything he owned to keep going. Today, thanks partly to Bernie, he is one of the richest men in Britain and has been honoured with a knighthood. One can also cite the example of Ron Dennis, who started out as a humble mechanic. Today, Formula 1 is a fantastic show where the sport sometimes suffers faced with the financial side of grand prix racing. But without this little man at the helm, the sport would never enjoy the limelight it basks in today. Only the Olympic Games and the football World Cup gets a bigger audience than Formula 1 and in the case of these two events, they only take place once every four years. Grands Prix take place once a fortnight.

Entering the paddock at a grand prix is to experience a fantastic circus which only stays in town for four days. Thirty years ago, the paddock was not even surfaced and the cars were prepared on the grass or even in the mud.

Today, no one can fail to be impressed by the ranks of multicoloured shiny trucks and the

He receives the keys to the city of Budapest from the Mayor.

Family photos
With his Rumanian wife, Slavica and one of his two daughters.

1994 Pacifique Grand Prix.

futuristic motor homes. The clinical appearance of the paddock might not be to everyone's taste, but to Bernie, Formula 1 is a shop window, just like the one where he sold his motorbikes. Over seventy years old, his bank account now runs into billions of Euro and he is one of the richest men in England. To ensure the future of his family, virtually none of his businesses are in his name. FOCA which became FOA is now in his wife Slavica's name. The grand prix commercial rights are brought together under the name of SLEC, which is based on his wife's name: Slavica Ecclestone Corporation. He makes do with being a salaried director with an annual salary of 10 million Euro. Recently, Ecclestone had put a lot of energy into establishing a relationship with Australian press mogul Rupert Murdoch to back his pay-per-view project. But it has not really taken off with viewing figures being very low, given that the free channels offer too much competition. The major constructors, who put a lot of money into the sport, object to the idea of potential customers having to pay to see the grands prix.

At first the constructors offered to buy 51% of his business, but he did not accept the offer and took on board an offer from Thomas Haffa, the German who runs EMTv. He sold 50% of SLEC for a healthy profit. The German media group, Kirch also came to the table after EMTV ran into trouble. Thomas Haffa was forced to sell out to Kirch, who also lost a lot of money as digital TV failed to make a profit. Bernie offered to buy the business back to sell them on to the Grand Prix World Championship, the constructors' association, which wants to invest in the

sport and control TV free-to-view broadcasting. Their aim is to maximise profits and split them between the teams. If the bid fails, then they are threatening to set up their own parallel championship in 2008. Bernie is currently fighting hard to ensure that does not happen to ensure that nothing destroys the goose which lays the golden eggs.

Formula 1 is reckoned to generate around 3 billion Euro and this baffling amount proves that the little man still knows what he is doing and so sees no need to retire just yet. Formula 1 is his life. ■

Bernie with Juan Pablo Montoya, Michael Schumacher and Kimi Räikkönen, the three fighters for the 2003 F1 World Championship.

His private motorhome and FOA plane.

Pasquale LATTUNEDDU

The Grand Prix Stage Manager

FORMULA ONE ADMINISTRATION LTD.
Mr. Pasquale LATTUNEDDU

His desk is at the heart of the paddock.

They call him Pasquale. His name and image are unknown to the general public. His photo never features in the specialist magazines or on television. But in the Formula 1 paddock, everyone knows him. Working with Bernie Ecclestone for the past ten years, he is the man on-site who ensures a Grand Prix runs like clockwork. From Sardinia, in his forties, he is omnipresent and all powerful. His office is in the heart of the paddock and nothing escapes him. He arrives well before the huge transporters and motorhomes arrive at the start of race week. Pasquale orchestrates the parking of these mastodons of motor racing. The motorhomes, these havens of peace, welcome and rest have to fit into specific areas and Pasquale makes sure they do. White lines like those on a tennis court provide a reference point for anyone trying to steal a few centimetres. The gigantic circus takes about three days to set up. From Wednesday

night onwards, everything in the paddock must conform to the draconian rules he sets. As from Thursday, his office is easy to find as dozens of people queue up to get those much needed extra passes. This is yet another aspect of the sport he controls. Only the press with permanent accreditation from the Federation Internationale Automobile and team members escape this experience which is full of pitfalls. Unknowns are not the only ones who go through the ordeal as team bosses, drivers and team managers sometimes have to call on Pasquale's good grace to obtain additional guest passes.

Getting into the paddock is ever more difficult and a certain dress code is also expected. A while ago, a French photographer was seen sporting an ornate French beret, which earned him a ticking off as it did not meet Pasquale's standards. In 2000, Jaguar turned up at Silverstone with its brand new motorhome. On the roof leaped a huge

chrome big car. By the next grand prix, the beast had disappeared. It seems that Bernie did not like the idea of the paddock turning into a zoo, with the jaguar, the Peugeot lion and Ferrari's prancing horse. Of course, it fell to Pasquale to tame the big cat. If a motorhome chef tries to vary his menu by grilling some sardines, Pasquale will soon sniff out the fishy smell and get cook to rethink his menu, rather than have strange smells wafting down the paddock.

When a famous star turns up for the races, if Bernie is absent, it falls to Pasquale to act as guide and ambassador, introducing drivers and explaining the workings of F1.

But Pasquale's role does not end there. During the race, Pasquales cruises the pit lane, rounding up the small number of photographers allowed on pit wall during refuelling stops.

Finally, he also masterminds all the ceremonial side of the sport.

After final qualifying the top three drivers are weighed and it is his job to take them to the TV interview room and then onto the press room. Television waits for no man. On Sunday, he does the same after the race, leaving the winner just a few moments to savour his victory with his team, before Pasquale marches him off to the podium. It is a thankless task. Pasquale can be cordial and kind and while some might contest the rigour of his regime one cannot deny its efficiency. Some old hands criticise his methods. But the special guests are impressed by what they see. Formula 1 is supposed to be on the cutting edge and everything is done to maintain that image. A firm hand is therefore required. Pasquale is a fist of iron in a velvet glove. ∎

Philippe GURDJIAN

the track soon became one of the safest in the world and his organisational abilities were recognised. FOCA, the F1 teams organisation awarded him the trophy for the best organised F1 grand prix in 1991 and 1992. He then became a director of the circuit, a post he occupied up until 1998.

"At the start of that year, Bernie Ecclestone gave me an exciting mission to organise a grand prix in Malaysia at the end of the 1999 season. I was delighted to take up the challenge." The results were exceptional. In little over a year, Gurdjian created an ultra-modern circuit facility with futuristic buildings. Suddenly, compared with Sepang, all the other circuits in the world looked old fashioned. Once again he won the FOCA prize as the event was an undeniable success.

In May of that year, Bernie Ecclestone announced he had bought the Paul Ricard Circuit, with plans to turn it into the ultimate test circuit. "He wanted to build something unique." Once again, Gurdjian was put in charge and after his success in Sepang, he threw himself into this new task. The Castellet resembled a building site worthy of the Pharaohs. As a tribute to

He is a friend and close ally of Bernie Ecclestone. Well known in the world of motor racing, Philippe Gurdjian's career began in advertising. His passion for racing saw him take part in the Le Mans 24 Hours seven times from 1975 onwards. In 1979, along with Jean-Pierre Beltoise, he created NOSCAR, a French championship for touring cars and he was the cornerstone of its success up to 1986.

"During that time, I got to know Paul Ricard well, when he welcomed us to his circuit. He asked me to take on the organisation of the French Grand Prix starting in 1985." Under the aegis of Gurdjian, the south of France track, built in 1970, blossomed once again. The French round took place at the Castellet track up to 1990 and was always well run. In November of that year, he was confirmed as the organiser of the French Grand Prix at Magny-Cours. Thanks to his innovative ideas,

At the inauguration of the Malaysian circuit in 1999.

Paul Ricard, the central building was maintained, or to be precise its external walls only. Gurdjian had the interesting idea of building the pits on two levels, with a soundproof upper tier for the engineers: an idea which is bound to be copied in the future. Luxurious suites allow team guests to look down on the garages below.

Knocking down the old facilities began in February 2001 and twelve months later, the new Paul Ricard HTTT (High Technology Test Track) was born. Words are hard to come by to describe the new ultra-modern installation. The architecture of the buildings is certainly a success, but the real innovation comes from the fact there are 40 potential track layouts. On top of that, the surface of run-off areas are designed to produce progressively more grip to slow spinning cars, meaning that the

old-style gravel traps have had their day. This mix of different grades of asphalt is the very latest in safety technology, rendering the guard rails virtually obsolete.

This should save teams a great deal of bent bodywork. A lover of art and painting, Gurdjian got his pallet out to decorate the run off areas with long blue bands which follow the track, producing a startling effect, which he had first tried back in 1986, painting the lines at the side of the track in a sky blue colour.

Sunshine 300 days per year only adds to the appeal. Toyota has already set up a testing base there along the main straight and some other teams are expected to follow. Philippe Gurdjian is an indefatigable worker who puts in around 20 hours a day at the

office. At Le Castellet, he also built an airport and two hotels. The most prestigious, the Hotel du Circuit, gets a four star rating, built in a style halfway between Moorish and Tuscan. Just a few kilometres from the Mediterranean, it is a true haven of peace, fitted out with a health spa, a swimming pool and some golf holes.

In 2001, he was approached by the Royal Automobile Club of Catalunya and its circuit to help organise the Spanish Grand Prix. In 2002, the main grandstand doubled in size. Gurdjian is always in search of new Herculean tasks, with his endeavours becoming always more incredible and grandiose. Are there any limits for this genius of organisation, this F1 master builder? In mid-June 2003, the minister of works of Bahrain visited the Paul Ricard Circuit to see how it should be done and he was deeply impressed. ∎

A view from the new grandstand at the Spanish circuit of Barcelona. The same man has applied his touch to the Nürburgring and Hockenheim.

Hermann TILKE

He is not a well known figure in the sport. Hermann Tilke is a German, born on 31st December 1954. He is an architectural designer who has always had a interest in motor sport. He competed regularly in endurance races such as the Nurburgring 24 Hours and the V8 Jaguar Cup. Today, he attends around ten F1 grands prix per year.

After finishing his architectural and engineering studies, he set up his own company, Tilke Gmbh in 1984. Today, he employs a staff of 120 engineers and architects. While he works in several areas, his speciality is designing race tracks. "We also design layouts for driving schools, test

tracks and all types of industrial and commercial buildings. On top of that, we build stadiums and swimming pools and other sports venues."

But here we are primarily concerned with motor racing and Formula 1 in particular. In 1996, Bernie Ecclestone tasked Tilke with modifying and modernising the Austrian Zeltweg circuit which, for commercial reasons, changed its name to the A1-Ring. Next, Tilke and his staff were given a clean sheet of paper to design the Sepang circuit in Malaysia. This totally avant-garde facility instantly made every other circuit in the world look very old-fashioned.

Hermann Tilke talks with Bernie Ecclestone.

The magnificent grandstand at the Sepang circuit in Malaysia.

Tilke is the man behind the new main grandstand at the Barcelona circuit and the new layout and infrastructure at Hockenheim. He also worked with Philippe Gurdjian on the fantastic remodelling of the Paul Ricard HTTT circuit. Circuit architecture has come on in leaps and bounds in recent years and the indefatigable Tilke is now working on the new circuits in Bahrain and Shanghai, which are due to be operational in 2004. With no time to draw breath, he is then due to turn his attentions to Mount Fuji on behalf of Toyota in 2005. Apart from F1 venues, Tilke is also due to work his magic at the Norisring and historic names like Zandvoort and Estoril. Tilke and his crew pay particular attention to the environment around the circuit, concentrating on the architecture of all the circuit buildings. "We work constantly with the GPDA, the Grand Prix Drivers Association," added Tilke. "We always consult the drivers before validating a project and we pay a great deal of attention to their comments and suggestions. The design side of a project takes around a year and one has to count on at least a similar length of time to do the actual building, although the time taken can depend on the terrain and environment in which we are working." ■

Jean CAMPICHE

Born in Switzerland on 25th January 1945, Jean Campiche is a permanent fixture in the paddock. Having studied engineering and electronics, he tried his hand at motorcycle racing. For six years, he enjoyed himself in the saddle during the era of the Continental Circus and Giacomo Agostini. "I dreamt of being a works rider, but I never managed it. In Switzerland, there are no circuits and no constructors. So, when I was 28, I decided to try something else. I saw an advert for a job with Heuer, working with the Ferrari team, doing the timing. So I made my debut with Ferrari at the Vallelunga 1000 kms prototype race. I looked after timing for Ferrari for 14 years, including Le Mans and the F1 races."

In 1980, he fulfilled the same role with Longines, but decided to quit racing at the end of 1986. "I was worn out and needed a change." Then TAG-Heuer decided to set up a timing department. In 1989, he worked in skiing in North America. Then in 1992, the company became the official F1 timekeeper.

"I was back. I had to oversee all aspects of timing. This involved working with engineers, setting up the TV timing to help viewers understand what was going on. I am basically TAG Heuer's figurehead in F1. I look after public relations and the guests who come to the races. F1 provides the perfect image to help us sell watches, which makes up 99% of our business. There is no doubt that my best days in F1 were spent with Ferrari, in the days of Regazzoni, Lafitte, Mass, Lauda and Gilles Villeneuve. In the early days, it would take 20 minutes to produce a time sheet and there would be mistakes in the times and driver names. Once we had to change the grid four times. There would be protests and we had no computers. F1 in 2003 is less fun than in the 70s and there is less human contact. But the timing system has involved incredibly and for an engineer that is fascinating." ■

The Engineers

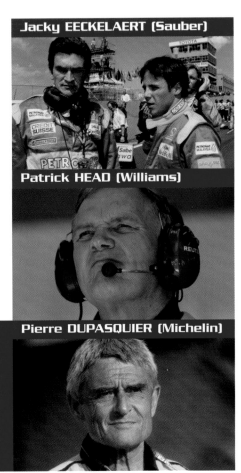

Jacky EECKELAERT (Sauber)

Patrick HEAD (Williams)

Pierre DUPASQUIER (Michelin)

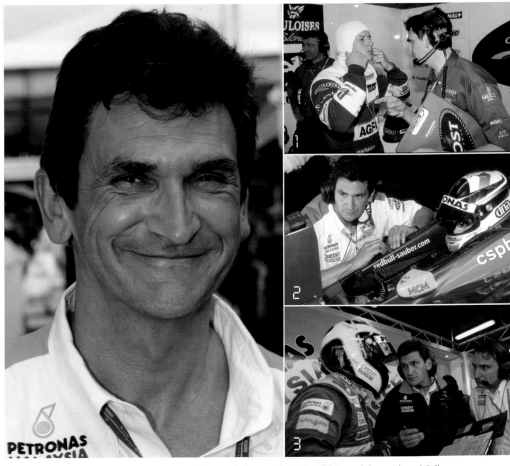

Jacky Eeckelaert with Olivier Panis at Prost (photo 1,) then with Kimi Räikkönen (photo 2) and Felipe Massa (photo 3) at Sauber.

Belgian Jacky Eeckelaert was born on 11th January 1955. "I studied mechanical engineering at the university of Louvain with the intention of racing. I started work in the Ford engine department in Cologne and in my free time, I raced in Formula Ford. Then I did a few Formula 3 races, but I quickly had to chose, as my job was taking up ever more of my time. I was contacted by one of the rival F3 teams who wanted me as their engineer. After a short period in Formula 3000 with Dams and a research job at the university, I devoted myself entirely to motor sport. I went first to Peugeot Sport then to Formula 1 with Jordan, Prost and finally to my current position at Sauber."

Eeckelaert is Sauber's racing manager with a staff of fifty. He also acts as race engineer for one of the drivers. He worked with Kimi Räikkönen and the young Felipe Massa. "I like working with young drivers. I like the technical side which is what I was trained in. But I also love the human side. The young dream of success and it is very motivating to help them realise their dream. It is a privilege to teach. A young driver lacks consistency and is less regular. But I am not a teacher. I just provide a list of things not to do and the traps they need to avoid. This year he is working with Heinz-Harald Frentzen, one of the most experienced drivers on the grid and he enjoys that too. Eekelaert has worked with a good number of drivers in his time. He has fond memories of his time with Ralf Schumacher at Jordan in 1997. "I had seen

him drive, but I did not know him. I like his approach to driving. He was criticised for being there because of his brother and people said it was all down to money. He silenced his critics when he made it to the podium in only his third grand prix. It's true he had punted off his team-mate Fisichella to get to third place, but it was still an amazing result. Ralf was there because of his talent not his money. Maybe he lacked his brother's motivation but he got there and has already won quite a few grands prix. Then, I had a great time with Kimi Räikkönen. I have to salute Peter Sauber's courage in listening to me. I absolutely wanted to have this young driver in our team. He thought I wanted to take him on as a test driver, but I wanted him as a race driver, when Kimi was still in

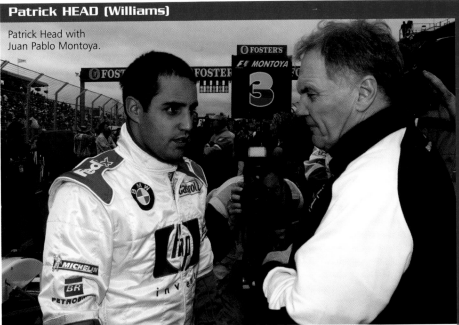

Patrick HEAD (Williams)

Patrick Head with
Juan Pablo Montoya.

Formula Renault. In the end, Mr. Sauber relented. We took a big risk as far as our sponsors were concerned back in September 2000. I had time to teach him. He was not out of his depth when he made his debut in Melbourne. One has to believe, but with hindsight I can see it was a big risk. This young driver who came from nowhere is the one who has surprised me the most. He was incredibly calm, always very concentrated and prepared to do his very best on Sunday afternoons and aim for points. Too many young drivers focus on their team-mate's times, but a qualifying time is not what interests me even if it is good for the team's status. It is much more important to be quick over twenty laps. When Kimi left for McLaren, we continued with our youth policy."

Jacky Eeckelaert regards his profession as a vocation and during practice sessions he is totally as one with his driver. He likes talking with his drivers, knowing what they feel, not only technically but psychologically.

A natural optimist, he does not dwell on the past, although he regrets the Prost episode did not come good. "I left before the ship sank. It was a shame as there were some excellent mechanics there who were devoted to the cause."

One can talk to Jacky for hours as his passion is contagious and he is an interesting subject, recognised in the paddock for his simplicity, his discretion and his kindness. He finds it difficult to have a family life spending twenty five days a month away from home as he attends races and tests. It is sometimes the price to pay in Formula 1. The price of a passion for racing. ■

Born on 5th June 1946 at Farnborough in Hampshire, Patrick Head is married with two children and lives in London. His wife is Maria Beatris Assumpcao, who used to be Ayrton Senna's press attache.

He attended races in the late Fifties with his father, who used to race Jaguar sports cars in his spare time. Patrick went to school at the Royal Naval College at Dartmouth and then studied mechanical engineering at University College, London. He tried his hand at karting and rallying, but soon realised he was not the most talented of racers.

He began working at Lola alongside John Barnard, working on cars for Indy, Can-Am and 2 litre sports cars. He then joined Ron Tauranac in the little Trojan team in F5000 and first tackled F1 with Tim Schenken. In 1977, he met Frank Williams through Walter Wolf, at a time when Harvey Postlethwaite was also working for the team. There was an immediate rapport between Williams and Head and the two of them set up Williams Grand Prix Engineering. With backing from Saudi Arabia, Frank Williams finally had the capital to put his racing plans into action. Head designed the first Williams F1, the FW06 for Alan Jones to drive in 1978. There were only 18 people in the team, which seems incredible these days. The following year, Clay Regazzoni gave the fledgling team its first GP victory at Silverstone after Jones retired, although the Australian would go on to win four times that year. The next year, Jones became world champion with Williams taking the Constructors' crown. Ever since, Williams has always been a front runner, winning a total of 9 Constructors' and 7 Drivers' titles.

The association between Frank Williams and Patrick Head is exemplary and the longest standing partnership in the sport and worthy of respect. Patrick is still as enthusiastic as ever and keeps a firm hand on his excellent engineering team. In an area where technology advances at the speed of light, it is amazing how Head continues to master his subject. He is now an emblematic figure in the paddock and the passing years do not seem to have lessened his enthusiasm.

He is also a blunt speaker, saying what he thinks with little concern for the consequences, even when attacking his own drivers. Ferrari's recent dominance has spurred him on even more.

Patrick Head with Rory Byrne.

The early days for Patrick Head and Frank Williams in F1.

Patrick Head with his wife, Beatrice.

Pierre DUPASQUIER (Michelin)

While there is little time for relaxation in Formula 1, sailing is also a lifelong love. "Over 25 years ago, before meeting Frank, I had built a 50 foot boat, which I sailed for about ten years before selling it. I would love to go ocean sailing again." But sailing round the world does not tempt him, as he spends enough time doing that in pursuit of his job. Every year at Magny-Cours it has become a tradition to see the leather clad figure of Patrick Head walk fly-spattered into the paddock, having ridden down by motorbike from England. In a busy schedule, it is one journey he always enjoys. ■

6 6 year old Pierre Dupasquier is a real character. The Michelin competition boss returned to Formula 1 in 2001 after his company had won world championships in 1979, 1983 and 1984 as well as winning 59 races. He was back to win the tyre war. "We wanted to prove we could make competitive tyres which were better than those of our competitors."
Dupasquier went to Michelin straight from college, before completing national service as a pilot. After the Algerian war, he returned to the Clermont-Ferrand company in 1962. His first project was Le Mans in 1965 with the

Renault Alpine. "Ten years later, our arrival in F1 was also done with Renault, although through a good relationship with Enzo Ferrari we carried out secret tests at the Fiorano track, where our radial tyre immediately proved competitive. Old Man Ferrari thought the results were encouraging and when I informed Francois Michelin, he decided to push ahead."

Michelin appeared on the F1 scene at the 1977 British GP at Silverstone, fitted to the "flying teapot," the turbocharged Renault RS01.

Ferrari also made the switch to Michelin and Carlos Reutemann brought the French firm

The early days in Formula 1 with Jean-Pierre Jabouille and Gerard Ducarouge of the Renault team.

San Marino 2001, the first win in this new area.

Pierre Dupasquier and Nelson Piquet reminisce.

seemed like the best means of showing off our technology. Michelin wants to leave its mark on F1."

In the space of 15 years, a lot had changed in the sport. "The tyre war is obvious. We are here to show we are at least as good, if not better than Bridgestone. It is a technological battle between two large companies and we have a great deal of respect for our competition. When we returned, we encountered grooved tyres for the first time. I think it is a silly solution and I was against it. On top of that, we did not have any data from the circuits so our challenge was something of a shot in the

dark." Michelin's first win with Ralf Schumacher was very important. "Ferrari was so far ahead of Williams that I did not expect any wins in 2001 and 2002, only a few podium places. Imola was really a great surprise as we won in style, with Ralf leaving everyone, including his brother, for dead." The passing years do not seem to have aged Dupasquier. "I will carry on as long as people feel I am useful. The chariot is still running so why stop it. I give myself another couple of years before moving on to other things which I have never had the time to enjoy, like reading and listening to music." ■

Pascal Vasselon, Pierre Dupasquier and Jarno Trulli.

its first F1 win in Brazil, on 29th January at Rio. The following year, Ferrari and Jody Scheckter brought Michelin its first championship title.

At the end of 1980, Goodyear pulled out and Michelin supplied the entire grid taking the championship wins. It too pulled out of the sport at the end of '84 with nothing more to prove. It was the end of act 1.

Then in 1998, there was talk of a return to F1. "Our industrial partners, BMW and Toyota told us they were planning to come into F1 and they wanted us to join them and as the sport is so popular in Europe where we wanted to strengthen our sales, F1

The Mechanics

They work outside the glare of the public spotlight and put an enormous amount of energy into serving their teams, be it day or night, year after year. They are totally devoted to their job. The drivers owe them a great deal and show their gratitude when they win. They deserve it.

Spain 2000. A mechanic's life can be a risky one. Nigel Stepney, chief mechanic at Ferrari is knocked over by Michael Schumacher as the driver pulls away from a pit-stop.

The Mechanics

Neil DICKIE

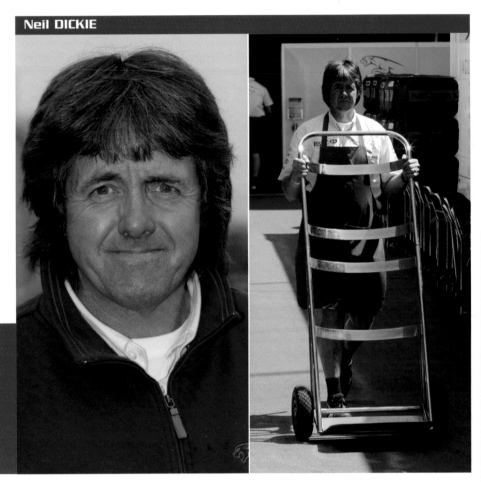

Neil DICKIE

"I look after Mark Webber's tyres. Along with John Gates who does the same job on the other car we look after all the tyres. When it rains that really adds to our workload. The new weekend format is good for us as we can now leave the track around 19.30, whereas before we were there until midnight at the earliest. I still can't get used to the idea of not having a warm-up on Sunday morning."

Aged, 47, Neil Dickie has finally made it to Formula 1 and he is a happy man. ∎

Massimo TREBBI

Mad about motor racing, the ever smiling Neil Dickie took his time reaching his goal.

"In 1989, a friend introduced me to Richard Lloyd who was running two Porsche 962s at Le Mans. I began as a mechanic on the Derek Bell/Tiff Needell/James Weaver car. The next year, I did the full Endurance championship with the Porsche Great Britain team. After that, I did a bit of everything and ended up on the BRM Group C project. I worked for them for nothing at Silverstone and Le Mans, but the team folded. I went to live in Toronto, Canada and went to see the Grand Prix at Montreal. I found a job for that race only, working for Keith Wiggins' Pacific team when the drivers were Gachot and Belmondo. At the end of the year, I came back to England and was taken on by Pacific, working at the factory doing a bit of everything.

I passed my HGV test but by then the team had folded. But Wiggins kept me on with the F3000 team running Cristiano da Matta. I looked after the truck, the fuel and the tyres."
But Formula 1 was still an itch that Dickie needed to scratch. He jumped at the chance to join Eric Broadley's Lola project. "Leaving for Melbourne, I was like a little kid. We had no time for any testing before the first race, but along with the drivers, Vincenzo Sospiri and Ricardo Rosset, we really believed in it. Our hopes did not last long as our Lolas were five seconds off the pace of the last qualifier. In Brazil, our cars were seized before practice and we went home in a state of shock."
But Neil Dickie's fairy godmother was keeping an eye on him and he found a temporary job with Stewart, which had just started in F1. "I had a two to four week contract as a stores person, then it was extended to six months. Finally, I was taken on full time."
So, in 1997, Neil Dickie finally made it across his personal desert and into F1. He stayed with Stewart Grand Prix and is now with Jaguar since 2000.

During the warm-up for the 2000 San Marino Grand Prix, the Ferrari team was having a last minute pit-stop practice. Michael Schumacher was a bit optimistic when it came to judging his braking distance and bowled over the mechanic charged with holding the lollipop to show him where to stop. Luckily Massimo Trebbi got more of a fright than anything else and to this day, he still waves the Ferrari drivers into place for their pit stops.
Born in Modena in 1955, he started his Formula 1 career with Lotus in 1987. He was

the motor home driver, keeping it shipshape and lending a hand in the kitchen. "I've got great memories of those days and I stayed with the team for three years and knew Ayrton Senna and then Nelson Piquet." In 1990, he switched jobs, working as a mechanic for the Lamborghini team based in Modena. I worked on the back end of Nicola Larini's car, whom I later worked with at Ferrari." After the birth of his son in 1992, he took a step back from racing, working in Maranello as a garage mechanic for the next

four years. "I joined Ferrari in 1996, driving one of the big trucks. Now, I look after maintenance on the Intertechnique fuel rigs. During the races, despite my little accident in Imola, I'm responsible for guiding in the drivers during the pit-stops and I also look after the fuel for Michael Schumacher's car." For Trebbi, Sunday is the busiest day. "I have to get everything ready for the refuelling which is a key moment in the race." With less work allowed on the cars, Massimo's day now runs from 7 in the morning to 9 at night.

"After the race, everything has to be dismantled and packed in the truck and we leave the circuit around 8 o'clock on Monday morning. There are two of us in the truck, taking turns behind the wheel. We are not allowed to drive for more than eight hours. Our furthest journey is to the British Grand Prix at Silverstone, when we do 1700 kilometres including a ferry trip. It takes us a day and a half." Once back at Maranello, Trebbi prepares for the next race, enjoying his job despite the long hours. ■

Modesto MENABUE

Born in Modena in 1961, Modesto Menabue walked through the gates of the Ferrari factory at the age of sixteen, where he started work in the engine department. That was back in 1978. "I've built some engines in my time, from the V12 Boxer to the turbos and then the normally aspirated V12s and V10s. They have evolved enormously in that time. The advent of

electronics changed our job completely. Research into new materials, constant performance gains and working on reliability are all fascinating aspects of the job." After twelve years good and loyal service at the factory, Menabue began attending the grands prix in 1990. "I only do the races, not the tests. I still work on the engine side. I study the telemetry and keep an eye on assembly and programming of the electronics. Since 1999 I have been working on Michael Schumacher's car. All our wins have been great, but the best was undoubtedly when Michael took the title in Japan in 2000, our first Drivers' title in 22 years. Winning the Constructors' in 1999 was also very satisfying."

Menabue has not really been affected by the changes to the race weekend timetable. "The engine department works in the same way even if the cars are in parc ferme. Studying the electronic programming goes on, especially on Saturday night." He admits that the paddock has changed a lot over the past few years. "It is much more stylish now and

the motorhomes are magnificent. I am happy to be part of it and if I wasn't I would have stayed at home a long time ago. It is great to share time with Michael Schumacher and I get on very well with him. Like Alain Prost, he is very approachable, always says thank you and always has a kind word, a smile or a pat on the back for everyone. In the past, I also enjoyed working with Ivan Capelli." ■

The Mechanics
Refuelling: a guide

The governing body's decision to allow refuelling to spice up the racing means that the trip to the fuel pump has become a key moment in the race, often deciding the outcome of a grand prix. This high risk operation is practised endlessly by the teams in race conditions…stopwatch in hand, nothing is left to chance. Wearing fireproof suits, balaclavas and even helmets, the mechanics tirelessly repeat the moves they will be expected to make without the slightest hesitation during the race.

Pushed in by two or three mechanics, the car must accurately hit a marker on the pit road. The equipment is universal. The fuel rig's rate of flow is strictly controlled and there are two gantries carrying the airlines to the wheel guns for changing the wheels. Teams might

do ten practice runs at a time, sometimes changing the nose of the car as well, while putting the fuel in is also part of the dress rehearsal.

As a rule, the decision as to when to call a car into pit lane rests with the team's technical director. Ferrari's Ross Brawn is a past master of this art, with several races won through a good call to a driver. Seconds lost cost dear, hence the endless practice. There is no room for human error and the procedure is also practised back at the factory prior to each Grand Prix.

When the decision to refuel has been made, the crew are all in place in the pit lane and a man waves his driver in with a "lollipop" before rushing to the front of the car to

control the procedure. The lollipop has instructions on both sides: "brake" and "1st gear." The front jack man controls exactly where the car stops while another rushes in at the rear.

One mechanic steadies the car, as the lollipop man tells the driver to keep his foot on the brake. When the four wheels have been changed, the car is dropped off its jacks. The driver is then shown "1st gear" and selects it. Changing all four wheels takes between 3.5 and 4 seconds. Each wheel involves three people. One removes the nut, another takes off the old wheel and the third puts on the new one, before the gun man, still on his knees, tightens up the nut with the gun. At the end of the procedure the gun man lifts

his arm to show the job is done. While this is going on, a man on each side of the car scrapes any rubbish out of the side pods which could affect engine cooling. One of them will also wipe the driver's visor. Refuelling is a delicate procedure carried out with surgical precision. The refueller locks the hose onto the fuel cell opening, both components derived from the aero industry, while a second refueller supports the weight of the hose, with another man on standby in case of technical problems.

A splash shield is placed between the refuelling and the rear of the car, to prevent any fuel spilling onto the hot exhausts and starting a flash fire. Mechanics also standby with fire extinguishers, ready to react in case of an incident.

When the fuel nozzle comes off, the lollipop is lifted away and the driver knows this is the moment to head back to the track.

Depending on the amount of fuel taken onboard, a pit stop lasts around ten seconds and whether or not the driver and team have opted for a one or two stop race naturally determines the exact length of time that the car is stationary.

There is a speed limit in the pit lane of 60 km/h during free practice and 80 km/h during qualifying and the race. A button on the steering wheel activates a speed limiter and releases the fuel filler flap. Depending on the teams, between 20 and 25 mechanics are involved in the refuelling procedure. ∎

The Medicalcorps

Sid WATKINS

Born in 1928, Professor Sidney Watkins is a world-renowned surgeon, in charge of neuro surgery at a London hospital. In 1978, he was asked by Bernie Ecclestone, then the boss of FOCA, to set up a grand prix medical service. Since 1970, Watkins had officiated at UK race meetings as a doctor and at the time, medical cover at the races was fairly primitive. In 1966, BRM team boss Louis Stanley decided to convert a trailer into a mobile hospital for the grands prix and for its day, it was pretty modern. Painted white, it bore the inscription, "International Grand Prix Medical Service." As the official F1 doctor from 1978, Sid Watkins became president of the FIA Medical Commission in 1980. Twenty years on, he is still there, still enthusiastic about his job. He never misses a race and every time an F1 car

is on track, he is strapped into the passenger seat of the Mercedes Medical Car. It has not always been the safest of seats. In Monaco, a couple of years ago, former F1 driver, Alex Ribeiro, charged with chauffeuring the good doctor, crashed into the barriers. Watkins emerged with a broken rib and a real scare. The medical car has followed the F1 cars off the grid ever since Ronnie Peterson's accident at Monza in 1978, when medical crews took too long to reach the fatally injured Swede. "Bernie then decided that I had to supervise all safety procedures at the tracks. I made my real F1 debut at the Swedish GP that year. I remember asking where the medical helicopter was and was told that as practice was less dangerous than the race, it would not be on duty that day! "Before I arrived, Jackie Stewart had really pushed for improved

Suzuka 1998. Charlie Whiting at the presentation of the new F1 seat.

More of a scare than anything else in Monaco, as Alex Ribeiro crashes the medical car into the barriers.

2002 Austrian Grand Prix: Takuma Sato has just been T-boned by Nick Heidfeld's Sauber which is out of control. In a situation like this, speedy medical intervention is vital.

safety and in fact Stanley's mobile unit owed a lot to his efforts. In Japan in 1998, with Jackie's team we presented the removable seat concept which is now in use with the aim of immobilising the driver when he is removed from the cockpit."

In over 20 years of service, Watkins has been through some difficult times. The Imola weekend in 1994 had a profound effect on him, with Barrichello's frightening crash, followed by the deaths of Ratzenberger and Senna. "Ayrton and I were very close for several years. We went fishing together and visited our respective families, so that he felt part of mine. We had a lot in common. Imola was a turning point in Formula 1, with Karl Wendlinger's Monaco crash and Pedro Lamy's Silverstone accident following shortly after. It was a critical time for motor sport." ■

Heinz-Harald Frentzen in the expert hands of Josef Leberer.

This quiet and unassuming Austrian was born on 30th April 1959 in Salzburg. Having studied for a physiotherapy diploma, he worked for ten years in the Bio Training Centre clinic in the mountains, around a hundred kilometres from Vienna. The centre was run by Willy Dungl and it was here that Niki Lauda was nursed to a remarkable recovery, stepping into his Ferrari cockpit at Monza, just six weeks after his terrible accident at the Nurburgring in 1976. "I was brought back to health by Willy Dungl, who was a physio and also a bit of a healer," said Lauda. "It was a miracle. He was a genius."

Willy Dungl, who died in May 2002, was the first person to look at all aspects of a driver's performance, including diet and it was with Dungl that Leberer learnt his craft. "I started working with Niki Lauda in 1985, as Dungl

had a contract to look after the physical condition of the McLaren drivers. Then I worked with Alain Prost, starting in 1987. In 1988, Willy gave me a new role as Ayrton Senna had just joined the team. I was very impressed at the idea of working in this team and I have to admit I had a moment of doubt about my abilities. I was worried I was not up to their level. It was impressive looking after these two great champions. I have extraordinary memories of those years 1988 and '89 when I was looking after the Prost-Senna "Dream Team." When Senna came to McLaren in 1988, he was not at all fit and lacked stamina. Prost however was in perfect trim. We worked a lot with Ayrton to make up the gap to Alain.

"Then, when Prost left for Ferrari, I continued working with Ayrton Senna and the other McLaren drivers like Gerhard Berger, Michael Andretti and Mika Häkkinen. I got on very

well with Ayrton. We were real friends. I devised a programme and then we would train together. I would give him massages and watch his diet. I went everywhere with him from Brazil to Portugal and spent more time with him than I did with my family. When he went to Williams in 1994, he asked me to go with him and I did, even though I enjoyed an excellent relationship with McLaren."

The collaboration between Joseph Leberer and Ayrton Senna came to an abrupt end on 1st May 1994 at Imola. "After the funeral, I felt totally lost and I did not know what to do. I went home to Austria and worked with the tennis player, Thomas Muster and the Austrian skiing team. A few weeks later, Ayrton's family suggested I return to working in Formula 1. Ayrton's sister said I had to be strong and that to carry on would be good

Riccardo CECCARELLI

Josef Leberer with Ayrton Senna after the Brazilian had won in Monaco.

therapy and a way of remembering the good times I spent with Ayrton. So I went back to Williams and finished the 1994 season. I looked after David Coulthard, Damon Hill and Nigel Mansell."

Feeling a bit like an orphan, he decided to return to the McLaren family in 1995 and '96, working with Häkkinen, Mansell, Blundell, Brundle, Magnussen and Coulthard. In 1997, he felt it was time for a change and switched to the fledgling Sauber team. There, he looked after training for Alesi, Herbert, Diniz, Salo, then Heidfeld, Räikkönen and Massa. "When one has experienced victory, it can be hard not to win anymore. It can be demotivating. So I am working with young drivers, working for the future. I have excellent memories of working with Kimi Räikkönen. He paid attention to everything he was told. It was a positive experience. At Sauber it is impressive what we can do with a small budget. The most important thing with the drivers is to have mutual respect as all these youngsters are highly motivated."

The passion for the sport burns in Joseph's eyes and at Sauber he looks after the whole team, not just the drivers. "I am still single," he says. "It is very difficult to have a family life, which is the negative side of the job. Before I retire, I would like to work once more with a driver who is fighting to win races, as wins bring extra motivation. But I don't think I have anything to prove anymore." ■

An Italian, born on 27th May 1960 at Viareggio, Doctor Riccardo Ceccarelli has been involved in the physical and mental preparation of Formula 1 drivers for the past fifteen years. Since 2001, he has worked exclusively for Toyota.

"In 1994, I set up a company called Formula Medecine. It specialises in providing medical and training assistance for the drivers. We have worked with over 250 racing drivers, including 36 in F1. The staff is made up of four doctors, five trainers and two physiotherapists."

Ceccarelli's first foray into F1 came courtesy of March Leyton House from 1989 to 1991. At the same time, he also looked after Scuderia Italia. In 1992, he worked for that other Scuderia, Ferrari. Next followed a long period with Minardi from 1993 to 2000, before switching to Toyota. During that time, his institute has invested heavily in research, working with the teams and drivers. ■

The Suppliers
The Helmets

The helmet is the only means of distinguishing one driver from another and usually the drivers stick to one design throughout their career. In 2003, with the demise of the Italian make Bieffe, most of the drivers are split between three brands: Bell, Arai and Schuberth.

Schuberth is the latest brand to enter the arena, starting in 2000. The company specialises in motorcycle and military helmets and did not really market its brand. It is part of the BMW galaxy of companies and Nick Heidfeld was the first to use it, followed by the Schumacher brothers, Ralf first, then Michael. This year, to simplify the job of wind tunnel testing, Rubens Barrichello uses the same brand as his illustrious team-mate. Depending on his status and the terms of the contract, each driver gets a certain number of

helmets per year. For several years, some drivers including Michael Schumacher and Jacques Villeneuve have new helmets for each event. The back of the helmet features a flag and the year for identification purposes. But not all the drivers are treated this well, some of them having to make do with three or four helmets per season.

Helmets on the 2003 grid
• **Bell** (4 drivers):
Villeneuve, Button, Panis and Trulli.
• **Arai** (12 drivers):
Coulthard, Räikkönen, Montoya, Alonso, Frentzen, Fisichella, Firman, Webber, Pizzonia, Verstappen, Wilson and Da Matta.
• **Schuberth** (4 drivers):
M. Schumacher, Barrichello, R. Schumacher and Heidfeld.

Bell's Tom Castermans, Arai's Peter Burger and Henning Blanke are on hand to see to the needs of their customers.

In the past, even the top drivers did not change helmets that often. For example, from the moment Jackie Stewart first used a full-face helmet in 1969, he only used three to the end of his career in 1973.
It was in 1967 that Bell invented the full-face helmet at its Rantoul factory in Illinois, USA. Dan Gurney was the first to race with one in the Indianapolis 500. Jacky Ickx was the first use one in Formula 1 at the 1968 Mexico Grand Prix. Given the prestige of Formula 1, badly painted and chipped helmets would not be the done thing in the paddock.
Today, the situation has evolved considerably. Following Michael Schumacher's example, the drivers have become very demanding with

A helmet has to withstand a greater weight than that of a person.

nothing left to chance. Comfort and the problems of high speed turbulence are constantly being evaluated.

In the past, drivers could be seen diligently cleaning their visors or changing them, using big screwdrivers. All that is history. The technicians arrive on Thursday, fitting radios into the new helmets, fixing the visors, clear or tinted according to their customers' wishes. Then tear-offs are attached to the visors. By removing these during the course of the race, the driver is left with a perfectly clean visor again. Drivers request different numbers of these. For example, Villeneuve demands three, while Schumacher only uses two. The type of visor and number of tear-offs can depend on the weather with yellow visors being used for rainy conditions. After each practice session, the helmets are cleaned, and a new visor and tear-offs fitted. Some circuits do more damage to the helmets than others and the gravel traps at Hockenheim are particularly hard on them. The visors are developed in the laboratory to withstand an impact at a speed of 500 km/h. They are tested with guns or heavy weights dropped onto them. In 1972, the rules were not so strict. At the French Grand Prix at Charade, the Austrian driver Helmut Marko lost an eye when a piece of debris was thrown up by the car in front.

Helmets must also withstand very high temperatures in case of fire and helmets have to pass all these tests before being approved

for the yellow sticker bearing the Snell SA 2000 standard. The helmet engineers carry out their work in the teams' trucks, while a team member is responsible for looking after the helmets, radios, balaclavas and gloves.

At the start of 2002, it was revealed that Michael Schumacher's Schuberth helmet had been designed after over 3000 hours in a wind tunnel. Its aerodynamic characteristics were blended in to suit a 2002 Ferrari lent by the Scuderia. It is estimated that one of these helmets is worth around 13,000 Euro. While safety is paramount with a helmet, its artwork is also very important. The Bell helmets are painted at Bell Racing Europe in Brussels, by Stephane and Martine Cohen, the importers.

It takes around a week to prepare a helmet with long drying periods between the 12 hours it takes to apply each coat. The basic shell used by Bell is worth around 2500 Euro.

At Arai, Mike Fairholme is the Englishman who looks after helmet decoration for all the contracted drivers. The Japanese company is happy to sell replicas, so that anyone with 1500 Euro to spare can have the same helmet design as Juan Pablo Montoya or Kimi Raikkonen, while a visor costs 120 Euro.

There is little difference in weights between the various makes, with most of them between the 1100 and 1300 grammes mark. Any lighter would compromise safety.

2003 helmets.

Cristiano Da Matta

Olivier Panis

Jos Verstappen

Justin Wilson

Jacques Villeneuve

Jenson Button

Mark Webber

Antonio Pizzonia

Giancarlo Fisichella

Ralph Firman

Heinz-Harald Frentzen

Nick Heidfeld

Fernando Alonso

Jarno Trulli

Kimi Räikkönen

David Coulthard

Juan Pablo Montoya

Ralf Schumacher

Rubens Barrichello

Michael Schumacher

New design for Trulli's helmet.

Once a helmet has been worn by a driver, it becomes a collector's item and the prices are rising. In 1995, an Ayrton Senna helmet went at auction for over 80,000 Euro and a Schumacher helmet is worth around 20,000 Euro. If your budget does not stretch to that, then replicas are available for between 1000 and 3000 Euro.

Each driver signs a contract with one of these manufacturers. Once again, Michael Schumacher does the best deals, with a retainer and percentage of the replica sales. The majority have less remunerative contracts worth a couple of hundred thousand Euro, so in F1 terms, it is not a big deal.

Tom Castermans is Bell Racing Europe's man at the track. "I am the link with our drivers. Generally, we try and have at least three helmets ready for each event: one for the race, one spare and one for rainy conditions, the latter having different ventilation and tear-offs. We modify the helmets from one race to the next, especially in terms of ventilation. Depending on the circuits, drivers like to have air blowing at their mouth, above the eyes or on the nose. Sometimes, they want all the air holes blocked off. In Malaysia, they obviously want the maximum in terms of ventilation and we can direct its flow by placing small parts inside." ■

The Formula 1 Tailors

The first firesuits appeared in 1963, light blue in colour and made in England. In theory, they were fireproof, but lost much of their effectiveness after being washed. In 1968, Monza's Mario Alquati created the Linea Sport suits, bearing a hunting horn as its emblem. Made entirely by hand, they were produced by an army of seamstresses working at home and the brand had considerable success.

"All the drivers wore them, except Stewart and Cevert, who had a contract with the American Naza company. The Nomex material was very fire resistant and it helped to save Clay Regazzoni when his car caught fire in South Africa. In 1975, we set up HP Maxessoires. This new product was made using two layers of Nomex and an extra proofed layer. Niki Lauda was wearing one of these suits when he had his accident at the Nurburgring in 1976 and in fact, his burns were caused by the fact his helmet came off. At the time, a suit cost 500

Euro and a driver used two per year. My wife Lori did all the measurements, sewed the name badges and the logos which were all done by hand. She supervised the manufacture which was all done by individuals. There was no factory as such." Mario, who is still based in Monza, looked after the business side. Then, at the start of the 80s, the major manufacturers arrived: Simpson from the United States and Stand 21 from Dijon in France dominated the market. Mario Alquati and his wife were forced to throw in the towel. Then, the drivers began to demand a free supply and in recent times some are even paid to wear a particular brand. Stand 21 boss Yves Morizot refused to go down this ruinous route. The business has now come full circle, with Italian firms currently dominating the scene. Michael Schumacher is rumoured to receive a million dollars per year for wearing an OMP suit, made in Genoa.

Bruno VAGLIENTI (Puma)

A businessman who specialised in working in the Middle East, in 1990 Bruno Vaglienti, originally from Turin, decided to change tack. He took charge of all sports activity for Sparco, one of the biggest suppliers of motor racing fire suits. In the space of a few years, the quality of his products and his attentive personal service made the brand universally popular, with sixteen drivers, about three quarters of the grid, wearing his products. "When I became sports manager at Sparco, there were only six drivers on the books. We did a good job." Ever attentive to the needs of his customers, rival brands had to make do with the scraps from his table.

After a three year collaboration between Sparco and the German Puma brand, Vaglienti opted for another move in September 2002 and he took charge of

Puma's motor racing involvement. "Currently, we work with ten drivers, from Jordan, Sauber, Jaguar, Toyota and Minardi. In the case of Sauber and Minardi, we also supply all the mechanics' fire suits. Sauber and Jordan also wear Puma shirts, trousers and shoes. It's a new challenge and a new beginning for me."

Apart from delivering suits to the circuits, he is there to take new orders from the teams and sort out any problems with ill fitting suits. "A driver gets through twenty made to measure suits per year. The most demanding is definitely Ralf Firman, because he is a tight fit in the cockpit of his Jordan. We also supply around fifty suits per year to the teams. Sauber and Minardi do not carry any tobacco sponsorship, so we do not have to produce

different suits for grands prix where tobacco advertising is banned. Each driver uses around thirty pairs of gloves in a season. A suit costs around 1500 Euro and shoes are 150 a pair and 100 for a pair of gloves. All our suits are made in Turin, the Silicone Valley of the business. The shoes are made in Taiwan where we have a research and development department. We need to be able to react very quickly from one grand prix to another."

49 year old Vaglienti still lives in Turin and travels to all the races and some of the tests. Puma is not just involved in Formula 1, as it supplies the Newman-Haas Champcar team, and the Ganassi and Rahal crews in IRL. ∎

PJ RASHDI (Alpinestars)

While the Turin based Sparco firm has been around in Formula 1 for some time now, a new marque has recently found its way into the grand prix paddocks. Alpinestars is another Italian firm and it is represented at the races by the American, PJ Rashdi, often assisted by Emmanuel Longobardi. Alpinestars is a well known name in the two wheeled world where it has enjoyed much success. As PJ says: "Our fame in motor cycle racing has created lots of interest in the world of motor racing. We produce suits, gloves and shoes, all of very high quality. The teams provide us with guidelines of the look they are after, dependent on their sponsors and their own

requirements, which we then study before coming up with suggestions of our own." Alpinestars is proud of the fact they supply thirty five top line racing drivers. "Ever since he was in F3000 and then in the States, Juan Pablo Montoya has stuck with our products. Today, we also supply the McLaren and BAR drivers, as well as the entire Renault team."

This brand has a young image and is currently a trend setter. Just as the drivers fight it out on the track, so too the tailors battle it out in the paddock, as Formula 1 provides them with a fantastic marketing tool. ∎

SidMOSCA

Special artwork for Rubens Barrichello's helmet, incorporating ideas from Ayrton Senna's. A way to pay hommage to the late Brazilian champion.

With helmets from Fittipaldi, Piquet, Rosberg and Senna, Mosca can claim nine world championship titles.

Rubens Barrichello is proud to carry the Brazilian colours.

Sid Mosca's is not exactly a well known name in Formula 1. The 65 year old has not set foot in the paddock for many a year. In Santo Amaro, in the suburbs of Sao Paulo, a few kilometres from the Interlagos circuit and helped by his son Alan and nine employees, he paints drivers' helmets and racing cars. He was a pioneer in this field and was the first to personalise a driver's helmet design.

At the start of the 70s, Cloacyr Sidney Mosca tried his hand at racing, in touring cars at Interlagos. The paintwork on his car caused a stir. As a hard up driver, he did not shine on the track, but as a painter he attracted a lot of attention from his rivals. At this time, he also did his first helmet design for Emerson Fittipaldi. At the time, few drivers gave their

helmet colour scheme much thought. "Emerson Fittipaldi was my top model and he wore my designs to his very last race." When the Brazilian launched his own

Copersucar team in 1976, he naturally chose Mosca to do the artwork and paint for his cars. Soon, Brabham, Lotus and Jordan followed suit. Mosca is proud to show off the

The famous Lotus 78 with its splendid black and gold livery.

Artwork in celebration of the fiftieth anniversary of the Formula 1 World Championship.

Sid Mosca and his son in front of an enviable collection of helmets.

All the artwork is done by hand so each one is unique.

Sid's workshop is also responsible for painting Felipe Massa's helmet.

certificate given him by Colin Chapman as proof of having painted Mario Andretti's Lotus in the space of twelve hours. Unfortunately, this particular Lotus 78, in JPS colours, was destroyed in a fire the night before the 1977 Brazilian Grand Prix. That same year, he met a young kart racer called Ayrton Senna da Silva, who asked him to come up with a helmet design reprising the Brazilian national colours. All through his too short career, the design never changed. Sid proudly points out that drivers using his helmet designs took nine world titles: Emerson Fittipaldi (1972 and 1974,) Nelson Piquet (1981, 1983 and 1987,) Keke Rosberg (1982) and Ayrton Senna (1988, 1990 and 1991.) All the Brazilians who made it to Formula 1 have called on his services. In 1995, Rubens Barrichello asked Sid to design a helmet combining his colours with those of Ayrton Senna, in homage to the late champion and in 1999, Bernie Ecclestone commissioned him to paint 50 commemorative helmets to celebrate fifty years of Formula 1 history.

Mosca and his staff produce just 30 helmets per month, with quality and finish the watchwords. "The design of a helmet is the other face of a driver. It is a means of identification on track and without wishing to sound presumptuous, I feel I contribute to a driver's image."

Rubens Barrichello and Felipe Massa have their helmets painted by Mosca and it is not just the F1 drivers who use his services. Gil de Ferran, Helio Castroneves and many other Brazilian drivers have carried the colours of the flamboyant sorcerer from Santo Amaro. ■

The DriverManagers

Willi Weber (Michael and Ralf Schumacher) and Julian Jakobi
(Senna, Prost…) are two of the main players in the sport.

Julian Jakobi with
Juan Pablo Montoya.

Alain Prost with former
manager, Julian Jakobi.

Flavio Briatore is
delighted after his
young Spanish protégé
takes his first grand prix
victory.

What is the definition of a manager? A manager is someone who looks after the organisation of shows, concerts or matches or someone who looks after the professional needs of an artist or sports person.

In Formula 1, the five times world champion, Juan Manuel Fangio, was the first to employ a person in this capacity. Gian Bertone was in charge of negotiating contracts and start money for the Argentine champion. In 1955, Fangio received 100,000 dollars from Mercedes for the season. It was a record at the time. In 1956, he became world champion for a fourth time and Gian Bertone

proved a tough negotiator when it came to trying for a transfer to Ferrari. When Enzo Ferrari refused to meet his demands, Fangio ended up at Maserati. Stirling Moss also had a manager, Ken Gregory and in 1958, a rising English star called Stuart Lewis-Evans put his career in the hands of a certain Bernie Ecclestone, before being tragically killed in the Moroccan Grand Prix.

In 1965, an American lawyer from Cleveland, Mark H. McCormack set up a management agency called IMG (International Management Group) and tennis star Rod Laver, skiier Jean-Claude Killy and Jackie Stewart were among his first clients. Back in business, Bernie Ecclestone took charge of the affairs of the

Scottish driver's greatest rival, Jochen Rindt. Once again, this relationship came to a tragic conclusion, when Rindt was killed at Monza on 5th September 1970.

Following this fatality, Bernie abandoned driver management and turned to running a team before going on to create FOCA, which looked after the interests of the F1 teams. The last driver to benefit from Bernie's advice was Ricardo Patrese.

Niki Lauda was the first to create a real structure, with an office running his affairs. Without any outside existence, he managed to extract 2 million dollars from Ron Dennis in 1980.

Jacques Villeneuve with Craig Pollock.

Jenson Button's manager, John Byfield.

In those days, Alain Prost and Ayrton Senna were on McCormack's books. The British lawyer, Julian Jacobi personally looked after both these drivers, eventually working full time for Senna. These days it is virtually impossible to make a career as a driver without management support. As Bernard Cahier, an eminent journalist and photographer in the 50s and 60s so pertinently put it, "Suddenly, managers popped out of the ground like mushrooms." Managers boosted the rate card dramatically. Without McCormack, Jackie Stewart would never have got $100,000 out of Elf, Ford and Dunlop. Later, Jacobi's skills allowed Senna to pick up $8 million when he joined McLaren in 1988.

In modern times, only Niki Lauda, Gerhard Berger and Nigel Mansell ran their own business careers. The British champion proved the most adept at this, given that he is estimated to have picked up 80 million dollars

in 15 years of F1 and Indy Car. He was the exception that proved the rule.

Some managers prefer to remain anonymous, hardly ever coming to the race tracks, while others follow their protégé's every move. Managers come from all walks of life, with many of them coming from a legal or business background. But there are no fixed rules in this job. The former Finnish world champion, Keke Rosberg, even started to manage the careers of some of his peers before he had hung up his helmet. The most famous of those was of course Mika Häkkinen. JJ Lehto, Yannick Dalmas and more recently, Olivier Panis have all been part of the Rosberg stable. Rosberg's colleague, Didier Coton attended every race to attend to Häkkinen. Another example of the manager breed is Craig Pollock. He ran a private school in Villars in the Swiss Alps and he was a ski instructor to a certain Jacques Villeneuve. The

two got on well and they became inseparable. After difficult beginnings, Jacques Villeneuve's career owes a great deal to the management skills of Craig Pollock. Others involve members of their family. Jean Alesi's business affairs were handled by his brother Jose and for many years, Olivier Panis entrusted the business side of his life to his wife Anne. Along with his other duties, Flavio Briatore finds time to run the careers of Giancarlo Fisichella, Jarno Trulli, Mark Webber and Fernando Alonso.

The explosion of merchandising driver branded items has given the managers plenty of work and a means of picking up considerable sums of money for their efforts. Just how much money these men and women earn is shrouded in mystery, but the current king is undoubtedly Willi Weber.

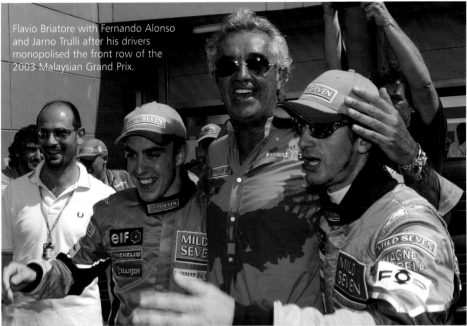

Flavio Briatore with Fernando Alonso and Jarno Trulli after his drivers monopolised the front row of the 2003 Malaysian Grand Prix.

Heinz-Harald Frentzen's manager, Ortwin Podlech.

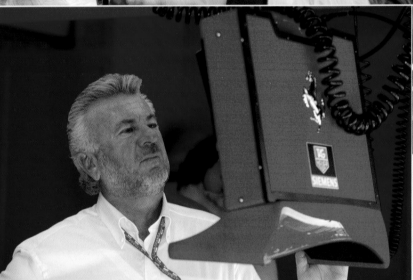

Felipe Massa with Ricardo Tedesci, his manager.

Justin Wilson's manager, Jonathan Palmer.

The managers of the 2003 drivers:

Driver	Manager
Michael Scumacher	Willi Weber
Rubens Barrichello	Frederico della Noce
Juan Pablo Montoya	Julian Jakobi
Ralf Schumacher	Willi Weber
David Coulthard	Martin Brundle
Kimi Raïkkönen	Steve et David Robertson
Jarno Trulli	Flavio Briatore
Fernando Alonso	Flavio Briatore
Nick Heidfeld	Werner Heinz
Heinz-Harald Frentzen	Ortwin Podlech
Giancarlo Fisichella	Flavio Briatore
Ralph Firman	David Kennedy
Mark Webber	Flavio Briatore
Antonio Pizzonia	Jayme Brito
Jacques Villeneuve	Craig Pollock
Jenson Button	John Byfield
Justin Wilson	Jonathan Palmer
Jos Verstappen	Huub Rothengatter
Olivier Panis	Keke Rosberg
Cristiano da Matta	Fernando Paiva

Willi Weber, business manager to the Schumacher brothers

An elegant fifty year old with a well trimmed salt and pepper beard and a permanent smile or malicious grin, depending on your point of view, Willi Webber is a permament fixture in the paddock. The owner of several hotels and the head of various real estate companies, his role is simple. He runs the career of the Schumacher brothers. For several years now, the five times world champion Michael Schumacher has been the best paid sportsman on the planet and as a talented businessman, Weber is tasked to exploit his driver's talent. Products bearing the driver's name, all part of the "Michael Schumacher Collection" bring in huge profits. Younger brother Ralf might not match Michael's track record, but he is still one of the best paid drivers in the paddock.

Be it Michael's championship titles or Ralf's race wins, Willi Weber is always there to congratulate his drivers.

"I met Michael when he was racing in Formula Ford and Formula Konigg. It was at the end of 1988. I could see he was really something special. I offered him a test drive in one of my Formula 3 cars. I told him if the test went well, he could drive for my team. At the time, a full season cost around 300,000 Euro. Michael did not have a bean. I suggested financing his season to help him get to the top. But I never dreamt of becoming a driver manager. At the time, we never spoke of Formula 1, we just moved up one step at a time. I therefore provided him with the means to succeed in return for a percentage of his salary when he finally made it." In the paddock, Weber is known as "Mr. 20%. Of course, the man himself strongly denies this figure!

It is reckoned that in 2003, the German businessman picked up 260 million dollars. He heads Julian Jacobi, another front runner in the game and Craig Pollock. Behind them come Enrico Zanarini, Keke Rosberg and Flavio Briatorie.

After Formula 3, Michael Schumacher joined the Sauber-Mercedes school, racing in Group C, where he teamed up with Frentzen and Wendlinger. He cut his teeth with these very powerful cars, while Weber looked for any possible route to Formula 1, the final step on the ladder.

"In the summer of 1991, I heard that Jordan's Bertrand Gachot was in trouble with the British legal system over an altercation with a London taxi driver," he said with a twinkle in his eye. "I knew Eddie Jordan well from the days when he ran an F3 team." When Gachot was imprisoned, he called Jordan and said: "I've got the best driver to replace Gachot at Spa. Schumacher knows the track by heart. It's like his back garden."

Despite Weber's enthusiasm, the wily old Irish fox Eddie Jordan seemed sceptical. "Spa is dangerous and no place to make your F1 debut." After some persuasive words from Weber and cash from Mercedes, he finally agreed, even wanting to tie Schumacher to a long term contract. Weber recalls: "Michael was racing at the Nurburgring with Sauber that weekend and I told him I had found him an F1 drive."

The fact that Jordan had signed an engine supply deal with Yamaha for 1992 did not excite Weber. Immediately after the Belgian Grand Prix, he met Benetton boss, Flavio Briatore. "In under an hour of discussions, Michael Schumacher's future with Benetton was sealed," said Weber with pride. The road to success had opened up.

But there was more than one Schumacher and a few years later, Ralf started out in motor racing. After going through the usual time in karts at the family's track in Kerpen, he joined Willi Weber's F3 team.

"After Formula 3, when Ralf went to try his luck in Formula Nippon, Japan's version of F3000, I sold my F3 team and concentrated on managing the Schumacher brothers' careers." This was done under the names of "Willi Weber Management" and "PPM Merchandising" which between them employ no less than 160 staff.

In 1993, after learning his trade, Michael Schumacher was fighting with the giants of the sport like Senna and Prost. Germany had never had a Formula 1 champion and regarded Schumi as its prophet. The German became incredibly popular. It was the opportune moment to set up the "Michael Schumacher Collection." The famous cap, bought and worn by millions of fans around the world, is the best selling item in the range and is a gold mine. But of course, no figures are available as to the profits involved.

It is now more than ten years that Willi Weber juggles his various business interests and it seems that his interest might be waning. "Up to 1988, I attended all the grands prix. For the past two years, I only attend the important races, coming to about half the grands prix." When asked if he plans to continue for much longer in this highly lucrative role, he smiles. "I'm beginning to get tired. I am helping two or three young German drivers, but I will stop when Ralf's career comes to an end, probably shortly after Michael retires." Willi Weber's success has been phenomenal and he is the ultimate reference point when it comes to driver management. He had the foresight and the genius to pick up the Schumacher brothers and that probably only represents a fraction of his talent. ∎

The Marshals

Monza 2000.

They are not usually in the spotlight, but during the 2000 Italian Grand Prix at Monza, one of their number died, paying the price for his passion for the sport. A few months later in Melbourne, F1 suffered another fatality.

In the paddock, they along with a few officials are the only unpaid members of the grand prix circus. In a world where money flows like water, marshals play a key role in the organisation of a race. The fact they are unpaid is a paradox and an anachronism. Not only are the marshals not paid, but they have to cover all their own expenses with accommodation and transport entirely down to them.

There are some rare exceptions. In Germany, at the Nurburgring, the organising club, the powerful Automobil Club Von Deutschland covers their costs. At Silverstone, the RAC hands out a small allowance. In Belgium, the RACB hands out 25 Euro per weekend and in Hungary, the marshals are paid 10 Euro per day and have their accommodation costs covered. Sometimes, at Magny-Cours and Spa, they get a grandstand seat for a friend. The organisers of other events do not see the need to open the moneybox. Some circuits dish out lunch boxes and drinks, but this is the exception rather than the rule. So what prompts people to get involved in motor racing at their own expense? One of their number, who preferred to remain anonymous, offered this explanation. "The only motivation is our love of the sport. It means we are part of the race and doing something. We are a necessary element. Being behind the barriers or in a grandstand is just not the same. For example, we might be posted at the Raidillon

at Spa or at the end of the Adelaide straight at Magny-Cours and each is different. You can feel the adrenalin rush and the feelings are different at each post at a circuit.
"In fact, one feels part of the event," continues our anonymous source. "You really have to be committed to it, as you are never thanked for your efforts. Sometimes you have to get up at 5 in the morning to spend the whole day out in the sun or rain and it is a costly hobby to pursue. But there is a good buzz between us. It is high spirited and we are like a big family. The drivers are quite nice towards us. Of course there is an element of risk, as we are not very well protected, especially if a car comes over the barrier. The most dangerous situation is when a part of a car, such as a wheel or wing comes off. But Formula 1 is not the most dangerous category from our point of view."

This year, marshals have to ensure that no one touches the cars in parc ferme.   In Monaco, the marshals play a vital role.

New flag with luminous signs.

There are around 200 marshals around the track at any given grand prix, of which 5% are women. They are not allowed at Monaco, where they are barely tolerated as part of the Red Cross! There are around 20 marshals working in the pit lane.

How does one become a marshal?

In France, one needs a license from the FIA which involves passing an exam and a minimum of three events per year must be attended in order to keep it. It is valid for all forms of competition, from the smallest hillclimb to the heights of Formula 1.

In order to be eligible to work at a grand prix as a marshal, it is necessary to officiate at 5 international level events in the year preceding the grand prix. A minimum of 6 months before the race, the marshal puts in a request to his local club, which passes on the request to the national federation.

Marshals often come over from different countries, as some countries are short of marshals and marshalling abroad requires a further license and all expenses are down to the individual, so car sharing is a common form of cost saving.

The marshals have to be on site by Thursday, the day before first practice. After picking up the relevant accreditation each marshal is allocated a post, which are positioned at regular intervals so that each post is in visual contact with the next one. As an example, there are 25 posts at Magny-Cours.

Each post is under the command of a chief marshal, a second in command and further marshals depending on the potential danger of the location. For example, at the top of Eau Rouge at Spa, no less than ten marshals are in situ.

The yellow flag, indicating an incident ahead and the blue flag indicating that a driver is trying to pass another are always on standby whenever the cars are on the track. Each post has other flags to hand: green (clear track,) white (safety vehicle on track,) red (race stopped) and yellow with vertical red stripes (slippery track.) The chief marshal and the man with the blue flag are linked by radio to the clerk of the course. The black and chequered flags are for the sole use of the clerk of the course.

The FIA safety delegate, Charlie Whiting does a lap of the circuit half an hour before every practice session, to check that everything is in order and traditionally, all the marshals stand at the side of the track waving their flags.

A marshal's day at the track is a long one and often affected by bad weather. The day starts at around half past six to seven and goes on until after the very last race towards the end of the afternoon. It can be a thankless task. These days in Formula 1, the basic unit of money is a million. The organisers pay a fortune for the right to stage a grand prix and to set up the event. Should the marshals be paid, even if it is just a symbolic gesture? If the day ever comes when there is a shortage of volunteers, then someone will have to put their hand in their pocket to ensure the smooth running of the Grands Prix and motor racing in general.

For the time being, a large group of volunteers, motivated by a passion for racing, take time off work to indulge their love of Formula 1 by being part of the show.

A word of thanks would be the least of rewards. ■

Japan 2000.

ACKNOWLEDGEMENTS

Jean-Francois Galeron thanks Bernie Ecclestone,
who agreed to write the preface to this book.
He also thanks all the team press officers and all
those who helped in the task and who
contributed to the tales of the paddock.